HORRIBLE HISTORIES

ANGRY AZTECS

Terry Deary Illustrated by Martin Brown

■ SCHOLASTIC

For Aidan Doyle.

Scholastic Children's Books,
Euston House, 24 Eversholt Street,
London NW1 1DB, UK

A division of Scholastic Ltd
London ~ New York ~ Toronto ~ Sydney ~ Auckland
Mexico City ~ New Delhi ~ Hong Kong

First published in the UK by Scholastic Ltd, 1997
This edition published 2016

ISBN 978 1407 16699 5

Printed and bound by CPI Group (UK) Ltd, Croydon, CR0 4YY

8 10 9 7

www.scholastic.co.uk

CONTENTS

Introduction

History can be horrible. Horribly foul facts and fouler figures, dusty dates and dustier dead people, lousy laws and lousier wars.

Now's the time for a revolution - not the French Revolution, the American Revolution, or even the rotten Russian Revolution but ... the Classroom Revolution!

Of course, a revolution needs weapons. So here is a classified secret. A secret so terrible that it is only whispered in staffrooms around the world. It is the answer to every pupil's question...

What is the weapon that every teacher fears more than anything in the world?

No! It's not the smell of Billy Brown's socks!

No! It's not the taste of school-dinner skunk-burgers!

No! It's not the head teacher finding the brandy in the book cupboard!

It is … a question!

It is … the question 'Why?'

Try it for yourself … but only use the 'Why Weapon' against a nasty teacher who deserves it. And keep on using it till they break down and admit they do not know the answer!

Here is an example…

See? Not only do you get revenge on your horrible history teacher … you also start to explore the really, really interesting thing about history. The question, 'Why did people behave the way they did?'

If you can answer that then you can begin to understand the question, 'Why do people behave the way they do now?' And, in the end you answer the only question that matters in life: 'Why do I behave the way I do?'

Hopefully this Horrible History book will help you to understand a little bit about history ... but an awful lot about PEOPLE!

Terrible timeline

The good news is that the world won't end tomorrow.

The bad news is that it is going to end on 22 December 2012. (So I hope you're a fast reader, otherwise you'll be seriously dead before you finish reading this book and you'll have wasted your money.)

In case you are interested in how you are going to die I can tell you that there will be disastrous earthquakes. If the cracks in the earth don't swallow you up then the terrible shaking that your brain cells get will give you a fatal headache. (It might be a good idea to stock up on aspirin now!)

How do we know this cheerful bit of information? Because an ancient people called the Maya worked it out. They could read the stars like you can read the Sun (newspaper that is). And the stars say that's when the world will end.

These Mayan people were just one bunch of some remarkable old South American nations who were a bit like hedgehogs on a motorway – they didn't have wheels (they never got around to it) and were flattened by people who did.

The other interesting Central American Indians are called Aztecs and they lived in an area we call Mexico today. They moved in as next-door neighbours to the Maya (in Yucatan) and naturally learned quite a lot from them.

The Aztecs were the neighbours from Hell. Within a few hundred years they had made themselves the top tribe in Mexico. Nobody argued with an Aztec. Arguing with Aztecs made them angry. And an angry Aztec was awful and far from 'armless. In fact you'd be the arm-less one as they bit into your biceps.

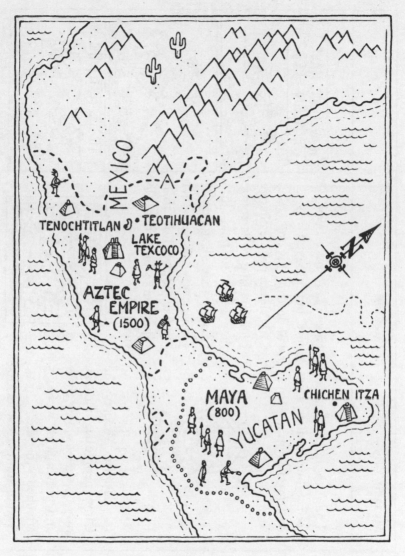

Time was very important to the Maya – their gods controlled time, which in turn controlled the lives of humans. Here's how time ran out for the Indian nations…

Date	Mexico	Yucaten
3114 BC	The fifth age of humans begins. There have been four other human races before but the sun has destroyed them in turn as it will destroy this one!	
1500 BC		The Mayan people change from hunting to farming; they begin to form into villages that all follow a similar way of life. (A bit like Millwall football supporters but not so vicious.)
1200 BC	In Eastern Mexico the Olmec people begin to take over ... they use war clubs and punch with weapons attached to their fists. Sort of stone-age knuckle-	

dusters! They sacrifice humans by clubbing them on the head.

Olmecs disappear! They leave behind pyramids and stone carvings and the calendar.

300 BC

City of Teotihuacan is built in Mexico with pyramids and a main road known as the 'Avenue of the Dead'. It's at least two miles long. That's a lot of dead!

200 BC

Mayan cities begin to grow with priests and kings having the power of life and death over the farming peasants.

Start of the great age for Mexico. In Teotihuacan they offer human hearts to the gods. In 1,000 years the Aztecs will copy this idea!

AD 150

The Maya begin to build temples which will grow bigger and richer in time.

Date	Mexico	Yucaten
AD 300		Start of the great period of the Mayan people. Lots of great pyramid building and cruel ceremonies.
AD 600	Teotihuacan is destroyed. No one is sure why or who dunnit! Mexico filled with lots of tribes and cities.	
AD 850	Toltecs arrive in Mexico – great artists and builders. Pyramids as big as the ones in Egypt, and metal. End of Stone Age in Central America, but still they don't have the wheel!	The Mayan cities are abandoned. Why? Like the disappearance of dinosaurs, it's anybody's guess.

IT'S MARVELLOUS TO BE MAYAN

I DIDN'T DO IT! HONEST!

HAVEN'T A CLUE

NO IDEA AT ALL

WHAT'S SO SIMPLE ABOUT FARMING?

SORRY WE'RE LATE

HOME SWAMP HOME

AD 1200

Now it's the turn of the Toltecs to be destroyed. They fall and their Tula City is ruined. Tribes from the north move into Mexico…

The Maya live on in small villages with a simple farming lifestyle.

AD 1300

One of the last tribes to arrive are the Aztecs. They are fine fighters. Aztecs work as slaves for the people of Colhuacan, but murder the princess (in the hope that she'll become a war goddess). They are driven out and squeezed on to an island in a swamp … but not for long.

13

Date	Mexico	Yucaten
1345	The Aztecs build a new capital, Tenochtitlan (now Mexico City).	
1367	Aztecs fight for the Tepanec kingdom and go on to conquer the valley for them.	
1375	Aztecs decide it's time to elect a king to lead them.	
1427	Aztecs getting too powerful. Tepanec lords try to destroy them but the Aztecs fight back and become rulers of the valley.	
1492	Christopher Columbus lands in America. For Aztecs life will never be the same again. It will be worse.	

1519 Spanish conquistador Hernan Cortés lands in Mexico and Aztec King Motecuhzoma welcomes him as a god. But by ... Hernan Cortés has conquered the Aztecs. It takes him just 2 years.

1521 First Spanish trips into Mayan lands looking for gold. They don't find it, and Mayan warriors kill Spanish leaders ... but they'll be back!

1542 Spanish conquer most of the Maya, but tribes in the jungle will give trouble for centuries.

1696 Some of last free Mayan tribes meet Christian missionaries ... and sacrifice them!

1901 Mexicans conquer the last free Mayan group. The Maya live on as peasants in the lands they used to rule.

15

The mysterious Maya

Nations come and nations go. They can be a bit like balloons ... they get bigger and bigger and bigger until suddenly ... pop! They disappear quite suddenly.

The first great group of people in Central America were probably the Olmecs[1] - they started a lot of the ideas that the copy-cat Maya and Aztecs would take up later ... courts for the fast and furious 'ball game', statues of gods and kings, pyramid temples ... oh, and the nasty little habit of killing and eating people. (Well, nobody's perfect.) Then the Olmecs disappeared. Pop! (It would be nice to think they ate each other all up ... but they probably didn't.)

IT READS: JUST POPPED OUT TO FIND SOMEONE TO EAT, BE BACK SOON

The Maya in Southern Mexico picked up where the Olmecs left off and built even bigger pyramids to sacrifice even more people. For over a thousand years they were the cleverest, most powerful people in the area. Then, in AD 900, their great cities with huge pyramids were abandoned. They were swallowed up for a hundred or more years by steamy jungle. Pop! At least, the cities went 'Pop!'. The Mayan people lived on as village farmers.

1. A few archaeologists are quite sure that the Maya came before the Olmecs. Some day they may prove it. But, even if the Maya did come first, it doesn't alter our story too much.

Further north in Mexico some of the strange Olmec and Mayan ways were being copied by the people of Teotihuacan (who went 'Pop!') then by the Toltecs (who went 'Pop!').

At last the Aztecs moved into the area, picked up a lot of Toltec ideas and habits and formed the last great people of Ancient Mexico. So, you see, if you want to understand the Aztecs you need to know a little about the Maya.

(And, by the way, the Aztecs didn't go mysteriously 'Pop!'. They were 'discovered' by people from Europe who came along and conquered them. But more of that later...)

The mystery of the Maya -1

There are two mysteries. Where did the Maya come from? And where did the Maya go?

Where did they come from? They came from Asia, across to Alaska (when it was joined by a frozen sea) and down through what is now North America.[1]

Like their cave-cousins in Asia they made flint weapons and hunted animals. Then they began to settle down and grow food and build villages about 3,500 years ago.

They would pray to their gods that the rains would come and the crops would grow. After a few hundred years they

---

1. This happened 50,000 years ago or just 12,000 years ago depending on which archaeologists you believe! For you and me it doesn't matter.

found some people were better at praying than others. They made these people priests – which was nice for them because they didn't have to do all that hard work in the fields. While farmers farmed, the priests prayed and worked out a fantastic calendar so everyone would know when to sow their seeds and when to expect the rain.

This was a great success. If the rains came then the priests said, 'We told you we were good!' If the rains didn't come the priests said, 'You people must have been bad – the gods are annoyed – don't blame us!' Anyway the priests became very popular and the farmers would take time off to build the priests bigger and better temples. They decided they'd be nearer heaven if they built them on high platforms.

In time (around 1,700 years ago) these platform temples became huge pyramids – then they built new pyramids round the old pyramids till they were as close to heaven as a pigeon on a pogo stick. The pyramids are deserted now but they are still there if you want to go and see them, trample over them and vandalize them the way tourists have for the past hundred years.

WOULDN'T THIS LOOK NEAT IN OUR LIVING ROOM

Hunters to farmers to priests. Simple, yes?

No.

Because some clever people came along, looked at the pyramids, looked at the native farmers and said, 'These simple farmers could never have built those pyramids!'

'So who did?' they asked themselves. (Clever people spend a lot of time talking to themselves.)

'The Egyptians built pyramids!' they answered themselves. 'The Egyptians must have sailed across the Atlantic Ocean 2,000 years before Columbus and settled in Mexico!'

Sensible historians said, 'This is all nonsense. Forget it. The Egyptians did not cross to South America.'

But on 1 September 1996 a sensational story appeared in the newspapers...

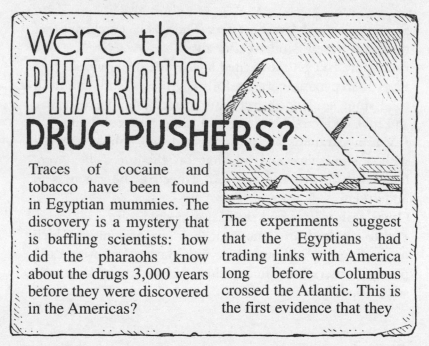

were the PHAROHS DRUG PUSHERS?

Traces of cocaine and tobacco have been found in Egyptian mummies. The discovery is a mystery that is baffling scientists: how did the pharaohs know about the drugs 3,000 years before they were discovered in the Americas?

The experiments suggest that the Egyptians had trading links with America long before Columbus crossed the Atlantic. This is the first evidence that they

Smoked tobacco or chewed coca leaves – the source of cocaine.

German scientist Svelta Balabanova did not believe the results when she tested the mummies from British and German museums. 'The results were a shock. I was sure it was a mistake,' she said. But she was convinced after repeating the tests.

The Keeper of Egyptology at Manchester Museum said, 'we have always said there is no evidence of links between Egypt and the Americas – but there is never any evidence until it appears.'

The discovery of silk in the hair of 3000-year-old mummies supports the claim that the pharaohs had trade links around the world. Cocaine has only been found in the coca plant in South America.

So there you are! A real mystery. There is just a chance that the Maya were Egyptians after all!

But before you get too excited look at the differences:

• Egyptian pyramids are carefully engineered and built from solid stone so they cover a tomb inside. They were graves, and took an incredible amount of brain-power to build.

• Mayan pyramids are piles of sand and rubble, covered with a stone face and an altar on the top. They were temple-platforms, and you didn't need to be a genius to build them.

Other writers have said the Mayan people were . . .

• Irish – the Irish are famous for their love of potatoes which originally grew in South America! Maybe they were early potato hunters who found their beloved vegetables and stayed there?

• Vikings – who, most historians agree, probably sailed to the north of America long before Columbus.
• Survivors from Noah's Ark – because Noah's Ark was built in America, some people say.

• Survivors from the Greek defeat of Troy - who floated over the Atlantic on the wooden horse, perhaps?

• Alexander the Great's Greek sailors – who turned right at the Mediterranean instead of left and became a little lost?
• Chinese - who turned left at Japan instead of right and crossed the Pacific by mistake?

There is, of course, one other explanation you might like to consider. In the 1960s a Swiss writer came up with a new theory. The beings who planned the Mayan pyramids weren't human. They were aliens from outer space! The pyramid platforms would make landing pads for their flying saucers! This may sound wacky and fantastic to you. But remember ... he sold an awful lot of books!

Horrible habits

Whether the Maya came from the Mediterranean or Mars, the important question is, 'Would they be the sort of people you'd take home to meet your mum for tea?'

Here are some of their curious little habits...

Miserable Mayan children

Children in Mayan cities had a hard time. Maybe you'd prefer to be a Mayan rather than a modern?

1 In a Mayan city there were two wells. (Well, well!) One was for drinking and the other was for speaking to the gods. At dawn a girl would be thrown into the water almost 20 metres below. At noon she was brought out and asked, 'What did the gods say to you?' Whatever she replied the Maya would believe. (Of course there was a good chance that she'd have drowned. In that case she would not be saying very much. Oh, well.)

2 When a Mayan baby was born the child and its mother had to be ignored for three days. This was so evil spirits didn't notice there was a new body around to attack. The mother would tie cords around the baby's wrists and ankles to stop its soul escaping. Tied up and ignored – even a teacher shouldn't be treated like that …well, not tied up, anyway.

3 The Maya had broad heads. Broad heads were common

and the Mayan lords didn't want their children to look common. They wanted to give their children narrow heads. How do you narrow a child's head? Strap boards to either side as soon as the baby is born and keep them bound like that for at least two days. The poor babies would have to lie strapped in their cradles – board out of their minds.

4 Other heads were bound so that they were egg-shaped with the point at the back. Archaeologists have found these strange skulls and wonder how the owners could think straight. But they seemed to manage and the priests were clearly very clever people – real egg-heads in fact.

5 Cross-eyed kids are cute. Who says? The Maya. How do you make someone cross-eyed? Fasten a ball of wax to one of their head-boards (or to the hair on their forehead) and let it dangle in front of their noses. (If my parents did that to me then I'd be cross-eyed and how cross I'd be.)

6 The children were sent out to collect the nests of mud wasps. The nests were full of the maggots that would grow to become wasps. The mud nests were heated up until the sweating maggots wriggled out. As soon as they did, the Maya would pop them into their mouths as a nice warm snack. (Try it some time. They'll give you more of a buzz than a packet of crisps.)

7 Boys would be taught to fish as soon as they were old enough. But the Maya cheated. They blocked off a stream with a dam then threw drugs into the water to knock out the fish. When the doped fish floated to the surface the Maya picked them out.

8 If a Mayan child died then its mother would cut the end off one of her own fingers and have it buried with the child! Pity the poor woman who lost ten children – still, she'd save on nail files.

9 Children were taught the importance of giving blood to the gods. If they couldn't sacrifice an enemy warrior then they could at least give some of their own blood. Blood was let out with the spines from a stingray's tail. In an important festival a Maya would give blood from the ears, the elbows and (if you were a boy) from your naughty bits! Oooof! Girls could instead pull a rope of thorns through a hole in their tongues. Owwww!

10 When a child was still very young it had its ears, its nose and its lips pierced so ornaments could be hung from them when it grew older. The wind must have whistled through all those holes like a bagpipe!

THAT SOUNDS LIKE SOMEONE'S TRYING TO PIERCE THE EARS OF A MAYAN *CAT!*

THANKYOU

It was a terrible crime for a Mayan man to run off with someone else's wife. If he was caught then the angry husband was allowed to kill the wife-stealer. He had to do this by dropping a rock on the victim's head!

Mayan lyin'

In the Ancient Mayan city of Chichen Itza there is a stone track over half a mile long. The track ends in a huge pit, 20 metres deep and filled with water.

A temple stands on the edge of the pit and owls are carved on the side of the temple. It is known as the Temple of the Owls (even your teacher could guess why).

There was an ancient story that said young girls were thrown to their deaths in the underground lake as sacrifices to the planet Venus. Nasty!

But when scientists dragged up dozens of human skeletons and examined them they found more than half were the bones of old people. (But don't get any ideas about throwing granny in the local swimming pool.)

So the story of sacrificing young girls was exaggerated. You can't believe everything you read … unless you read it in a Horrible Histories book, of course.

Did you know…?
The story of the sacrifices at the Temple of the Owls was told on a wall painting at the temple. But tourists had a

stupid sport of throwing bottles at the ancient painting. It is practically destroyed now. It's just a shame no one thought of throwing the tourists into the pit before they ruined the priceless painting for the rest of us!

April, Maya, June

The Maya created an incredible calendar that most of the nations of Central America copied for over a thousand years. They also had a form of picture writing (which other nations seemed to forget) and a system of numbers:

0	shell	7	•• over dash	14	•••• over dashes
1	•	8	••• over dash	15	three dashes
2	••	9	•••• over dash	16	• over three dashes
3	•••	10	dash	17	•• over three dashes
4	••••	11	• over dash	18	••• over three dashes
5	—	12	•• over dash	19	•••• over three dashes
6	• over dash	13	••• over dash	20	shell

Amaze your friends by learning this system. It's easy really. The dot is one and the dash is five. So four dots is four, three dashes are fifteen. A dot and two dashes is eleven and so on. The sign for '0' is a shell.

26

Now you are a Mayan mathematician, can you spot which of the following sums is wrong?

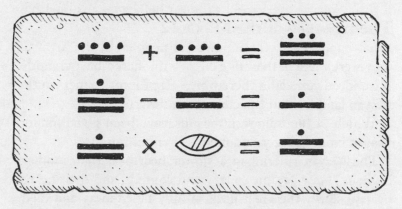

Answer: Did you spot the wrong answer? The third sum is wrong, so if you worked that out then you are right. 9 + 9 = 18; 16 − 10 = 6; 11 x 0 = 11... which is wrong, of course, because 11 x 0 = 0.

Years later the Aztecs were still using the bars and dot numbers to count how much people owed them! Why not use the system to claim a rise in pocket money? After all, it usually worked for the Aztecs (with a little help from a sacrificial altar, of course!).

Did you know...?
The climate of the Mayan land is very damp and warm. Even in the dry season the air is heavy with moisture. This can be wonderful for plants to grow in but very tiring for visitors from Europe. And it can also cause other problems. An archaeologist working on a Mayan city site had continual problems with his ear. At last he reached a doctor

...and the doctor pulled out several tiny mushrooms that had taken root deep inside his ear!

The mystery of the Maya – 2

What happened to these powerful people? In the AD 900s they were there in their fine cities with incredible pyramids. A hundred years later there were still peasant farmers in the Mayan lands ... but the cities were deserted.

Which of the following reasons have been given for the Mayan cities being abandoned?

1 The Mayan rulers had a slower heartbeat than modern humans. They became so lazy and content, and their hearts beat so slowly the great lords simply faded away and died. With no leaders the people of the cities couldn't work together. The working farmers always worked harder and were fitter, so the peasants kept going.

2 The Maya didn't know about fertilizer. Their fields became too poor to grow the food the cities needed. The lack of food caused the city people to move away and find new land to farm.

3 There was a terrible earthquake. The people thought this was a punishment from the gods and fled from the danger of falling buildings. They never returned.

4 There was an invasion from northern Mexican tribes. The invaders robbed the rich and executed them or turned them into slaves.

5 The peasant farmers became fed up with the priests. The priests did no work but took large amounts of food as taxes. The farmers attacked the cities, wiped out the ruling classes and then returned to their fields.

6 There was a terrible plague. In Europe the Black Death left cities empty as people fled to find safety in the cleaner air of the countryside. Perhaps the Maya did the same but never returned.

Answer: All of these ideas have been put forward. But they all could be wrong.

Perhaps the rulers really were aliens who one day got homesick and flew back to Alpha Centuri. The simple natives couldn't run the cities without their alien lords! The truth is, no one really knows the answer. It's yet another mystery.

The Mayan gift

Whatever happened to the Ancient Maya it was probably what they deserved. Because they brought to Central America the horrible historical practice of human sacrifice. In order to keep the gods happy they would kill their prisoners of war. The peasant prisoners would be turned into slaves, but the lives of enemy leaders would make wonderful prezzies to the gods. (Imagine our dear Royal Family being the victims of an enemy sacrifice! You would miss them ... wouldn't you?)

The sacrifice could be made anywhere but usually at a

temple pyramid and usually at a platform on the top of the pyramid.

The victims would be kept in cages while they waited to be sacrificed – some wall paintings in Mayan cities show these prisoners being tortured by having their fingernails torn out!

After ripping open the victim's chest and tearing the heart out, the victim was thrown down the side of the pyramid where priests were waiting to take the skin off and wear it to dance in.

Then bits of the victim were eaten. This was so that some of the spirit of the dead person could enter into the killers.

Imagine if this is true! Next time you eat a beefburger you could well become a real bull–y! If your mother feeds you pork chops then she can't complain if your room is like a pigsty. Chicken nuggets will turn you into a real bird brain, while fish and chips could help you win the next school swimming gala! Of course it sounds nonsense – 'Baa! Humbug!' as Mr Scrooge said when he finished his roast lamb with mint.

So, you see, the braver and more noble the victim, the braver and more noble the sacrificers became!

This Mayan religion was copied throughout Mexico and hundreds of thousands of people died. As late as 1696 the last free Mayan tribe disposed of some visiting missionaries by making them a ritual sacrifice.

Sort of, friar today, fried tomorrow.

Suffering slaves

Of course being a peasant prisoner wasn't much fun either. If you worked for an important person then there was a chance you'd be killed and buried so you could still serve your lord in the afterlife.

Long after the Mayan cities were abandoned, the idea of sending servants to the afterlife was still being copied.

Take the terrible Tarascans, for example. The Aztecs didn't conquer everyone in Central America. They didn't beat the tough Tarascan people for a start. The Tarascans were well organized and built strong fortresses that kept out the Aztec attackers.

They were also just as ruthless as the Aztecs. When their king died he was sent to the next life with all the people he'd need to run his palace there. The Tarascans executed and buried the following servants with the king...

ARE SURE YOU'VE GOT THE RIGHT JUG?

• the palace cook – she got the chop
• the king's wine bearer – she needed bottle for that job
• the keeper of the king's urinal who must have wet herself when the king died
• the keeper of the king's gold-and -turquoise lip-ornaments – who had a gilt complex
• 40 men-servants ... including the doctor who failed to cure the king's last illness (the other 39 probably thought murdering the doctor was fair enough).

Dreadful dentists

Next time you have to go to the dentist you should be happy. It could be worse. You could have had a Mayan toothache. If you did then here's the cure...

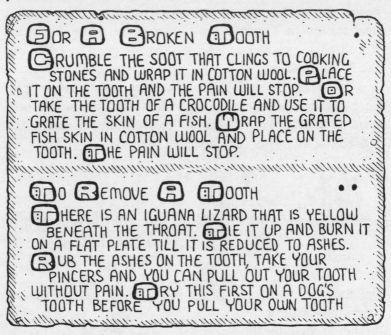

FOR A BROKEN TOOTH

CRUMBLE THE SOOT THAT CLINGS TO COOKING STONES AND WRAP IT IN COTTON WOOL. PLACE IT ON THE TOOTH AND THE PAIN WILL STOP. OR TAKE THE TOOTH OF A CROCODILE AND USE IT TO GRATE THE SKIN OF A FISH. WRAP THE GRATED FISH SKIN IN COTTON WOOL AND PLACE ON THE TOOTH. THE PAIN WILL STOP.

TO REMOVE A TOOTH

THERE IS AN IGUANA LIZARD THAT IS YELLOW BENEATH THE THROAT. TIE IT UP AND BURN IT ON A FLAT PLATE TILL IT IS REDUCED TO ASHES. RUB THE ASHES ON THE TOOTH, TAKE YOUR PINCERS AND YOU CAN PULL OUT YOUR TOOTH WITHOUT PAIN. TRY THIS FIRST ON A DOG'S TOOTH BEFORE YOU PULL YOUR OWN TOOTH

The superstitious Maya believed that even dreaming about a broken tooth was a terrible curse – someone in the family would be sure to die.

They also believed that starting any job on a Tuesday or a Friday was unlucky ... but the best time to plant seeds, get married or gamble was a Monday or a Saturday.

And the doctors weren't much better. They said that anyone who sneezes till their joints hurt will die within a day … unless you take a handful of orange leaves, boil them, rub the liquid into the feet and then all over the body! (Next time you sneeze you could try soaking your feet in orange squash. But don't pour it away and waste it. Take it to school the next day and give it to your worst enemy!)

Mayan medicine

Would you like to try any of the following tasty treats … even lf you were dying?

1. EATING BIRD FAT
2. SMOKING TOBACCO (TO CURE SNAKE BITE!)
3. SWALLOWING RED WORMS
4. EATING BAT'S WINGS
5. DRINKING A WHOLE BAT DISSOLVED IN HONEY WINE
6. DRINKING A LIVE TOAD DISSOLVED IN WINE
7. SWALLOWING A WOODPECKER'S BEAK
8. EATING DRIED TAPIR DROPPINGS
9. EATING SHREDDED COCKEREL FEATHERS

'If all else fails,' one Mayan medical book says, 'have the sick person remove one sandal, unnate in it and drink it.'

The Maya did all of these things. So swallow your cod liver oil and stop complaining

Did you know...?
The Maya lived in an area to the south east of Mexico that we call Yucatan.

But how did the place get its name? This is the true story!

The modern Maya

Since the destruction of the Mayan cities around AD 900, the Mayan people have survived in the south-east of Mexico. And they have had to survive some terrible tragedies in a horrible history.

When terrorists moved in to Mayan villages in the 1970s the poor villagers had to give them food and shelter. When the government fought back it was the Maya who received the worst of the punishments. Almost 200,000 were killed or 'disappeared'. Others fled and were forced to live in refugee camps in Mexico.

Mayan groups who stayed have seen their peasant farms destroyed and converted to huge cattle ranches to supply the Americans with beef for their hamburgers.

Maya who wanted to follow the old religions have been converted to Christianity ... and, anyway, they can't go back to worship their old temples because they are swamped with tourists!

Still, the Maya are increasing in numbers and are hopeful. A new king will awaken in the ancient city of Chichen Itza, they say. He will rise along with thousands of warriors who have been frozen in time. A stone serpent with feathers will come to life and lead them all in a great war.

Perhaps those tourists had better take their cameras and run!

The awful Aztecs

The Aztecs (who called themselves the Mexica at first) probably lived in the north of Mexico until they decided to move south some time in the AD 1200s.

They said that they ate some fruit from the tree of a god. The god was so angry that he made the Aztecs wander through Central America. They must have arrived in the rich valley of Mexico in the early 1300s where the people living there called them 'the people whose face nobody knows'.

The wandering, homeless Aztecs were defeated and almost exterminated by the Lord of Culhuacan city. The surviving Aztecs became slaves. But even as slaves those Aztecs were a nuisance, so the Lord of Culhuacan sent them off to fight a powerful enemy who would finish them off ... at least that's what he thought.

The Aztecs actually returned. The surprised Lord of Culhuacan said, 'You must have run away, you cowards!'

But the Aztec warriors opened sacks and poured out mountains of human ears over the lord's feet! 'These are from the enemy you sent us out to fight. We beat them!'

HELLO! WHAT HAVE WE EAR?

The story of the wandering is probably true – but what happened in the wanderings is most likely just Aztec legend. But there is something awfully, terribly possibly about the legend of the Princess of Culhuacan...

The truth is the Aztecs would have learned about human heart sacrifices from the Toltecs themselves.

But why cut out human hearts and offer them to the gods? Where did this gruesome idea come from? The answer is that the Aztecs believed a legend from ancient Mexico and followed its teaching.

Imagine if we did that! If we actually believed a story like Hansel and Gretel and then acted as if it were true. Then every time we came across an old lady at her oven door we'd push her inside! It sounds crazy but that's why the Aztecs behaved the way they did. They believed that old story.

What was the story? Well, I'll tell you if you promise not to believe it and follow its lesson. Are you sitting comfortably? Then here it is...

The truly terrible tale

Once upon a time there were humans on the earth. And the humans ate maize and they grew into giants. (Now, cornflakes are made from maize. So, when your mother says, 'Eat up your cornflakes and you'll grow into a big strong person,' then you know she is telling the truth.)

But even these giants weren't tall enough to keep their heads above water when a great flood came. It swallowed the sun and ended the first age of the earth after 4,008 years. Almost every giant on earth was drowned and turned into a fish. That's where fish come from. (Remember that when you next eat fish fingers. You are really eating dead giants' fingers.)

Still, two humans survived by climbing into a tree. They were called Nene and Tata and they started the human race off all over again in the second age. But, after 4,010 years, what do you think happened? No, it wasn't another flood. This time there was a great wind that came along and blew out the sun.

The wind blew so hard that humans had to cling to the trees with their hands and feet and even grew tails. They all turned into monkeys. That explains why the chimp in the local zoo looks so much like your Uncle Dave – they were both humans at one time ... at least the chimp was.

Again, two humans survived by standing on a rock. They started the human race off all over again in the third age. But, after 4,081 years, what do you think happened? No it wasn't a flood and it wasn't a wind, it was a great fire that carne along and destroyed the earth.

Of course, someone survived and started the fourth age and, of course, the humans of the fourth age were wiped out by rain of blood and fire. Nothing could grow and humans starved.

And that brings us to the fifth age – the one we're in now and the one that will end with earthquakes on 22 December 2012. (The Aztecs didn't have Christmas so they didn't realize how this will ruin everyone's Christmas in AD 2012. On the other hand you will be able to save money because there's no point in buying presents that will never get opened.)

At the start of the fifth age the gods met in Teotihuacan. That's a Mexican name that means 'The place where the gods are born'.

And it was dark. (Well, it would be, since the sun of the fourth age had been destroyed by the rain of blood and fire.) As you may know, there is only one way to make a sun, and that is for a god to set fire to himself.

Nobody wanted the job. Would you?

At last the boastful Tecuciztecatl said he was the greatest god and he really should be the new sun. No one agreed because no one really liked him. Still they built a huge bonfire and invited Tecuciztecatl to jump in.

The god looked at the fire and suddenly remembered he

was far too busy to become the sun today. Tecuciztecatl was Tecucizte-totally-chicken. That's when the wise and popular Nanahuatzin took a long run, a hop, a step and a jump and landed in the fire. Pow! The earth had a sun.

Tecuciztecatl was so ashamed of himself he too took a long run, a jump, a step and a hop and followed Nanahuatzin. Pow! The earth had another great ball of light in the sky - Tecuciztecatl had become the moon.

The gods were feeling pretty pleased with themselves when one of them pointed to the sun in the sky and said, 'It isn't moving!'

And it was true. Nanahuatzin had given his life to make the sun, now he wanted the other gods to give their lives before he would set off across the sky.

Of course they grumbled a bit at first. 'I wish he'd said that before he jumped in the fire,' one of them muttered.

'Well, it's done now,' another one said reasonably. 'I'll give my heart if you'll give yours!'

So, one by one, the gods came to the feathered snake god, Quetzalcoatl, and had their living hearts torn out of their bodies. When the sacrifices had been made the sun began to move across the sky as it has done ever since.

It was said giants built the pyramids of the sun and of the moon in Teotihuacan and the first leaders were buried inside them. The ruins of the pyramids still stood in Teotihuacan when the first Aztecs arrived in Mexico. The simple Aztecs looked at the pyramids, were sure they could only have been built by giants and they really believed the tale of the gods.

BUT ... the Aztecs said, 'If the gods had to give their hearts to keep the sun moving in the sky then we humans should do the same. We must make sure the sun is properly fed with regular supplies of heart.'

And that's why the Aztecs began sacrificing humans to the gods.

It's silly and it's savage and thousands of people died horrible deaths, all because of a story.

Did you know…?
A Spanish priest called Siguenza came to Mexico in the 1500s. He didn't believe the story about the gods of Teotihuacan. But he didn't believe that normal humans had built those great pyramids in the deserted city either. He had a different theory about the people who built the pyramids. He said some incredible people had arrived in Mexico from a huge island called Atlantis before it sank into the sea. And even to this day some people believe that's where the ancient Mexican rulers came from.

Swamp serpent soup

The greatest Aztec legend says they were led to their new land by a prophet called Tenoch. If the first settlers had written letters back to their old homeland then they may have looked something like this...

Dear Mum

Here we are in our new home and it's really smashing. Lots to eat. As you know, Tenoch the prophet led us down here from Aztlan and kept going on about a snake and an eagle and a cactus. He'd had a dream. Well, we all have dreams but we don't go rushing off with half the tribe to make the dreams come true, do we? Personally, Mum, I thought he was potty. But we pushed on until we reached this swampy lake. A horrible place, but the land around the lake was fine.

Of course the trouble was - you've guessed it - some other tribes already live on this land. Now I'm a warrior, as you know, Mum, but their warriors were bigger than me and there were more of them. "What do we do, Tenoch?" we asked.

"We talk," he said. "We ask them to give us some land"

If I thought Tenoch was a nutter <u>before</u> then I was <u>sure</u> he was a few bricks short of an adobe then! Ask! For land!

Anyway, we asked. The five tribes were ready with an answer. They had smug little grins on

their ugly little faces as they pointed at the lake.
Because there, in the middle of the lake, was an
island. They even offered Tenoch a boat to
go and have a look at it. So off he paddled and
came back a while later. "The snake, the
eagle and the cactus!" he cried. "It is my
dream! I saw an eagle, perched on a cactus
tearing at a snake it had caught!"

"Oh, yes, didn't we tell you?" the enemy
chief said. "The island is full of snakes!
Poisonous snakes!" he chuckled. That's when I
saw their sneaky little plan! They wanted rid
of us so they sent us across to a snake-
infested island so the serpents could kill us off.

They don't know the Aztecs! We jumped
into the boats and paddled there as fast as the
weeds would let us!

We jumped ashore and were met by the
snakes. Lovely, long fat things. And they'd never
seen many humans before. They just looked at
us with their cute little faces and licked their
poisonous fangs with their pretty purple tongues.
There was a funny sort of surprised expression
on their faces as their heads hit the ground.

The snakes were as simple as the tribes—
folk. They didn't know that a favourite Aztec
meal is snake meat!

So I can't wait for you to come and join us, Mum. Snake soup, snake stew, roast snake steak, minced snake burgers and spicy snake fry. I'm working on a new recipe myself. I call it snake and kidney pie.

So we've named our new home Tenochtitlan after the prophet. Still, I have a feeling we won't be staying here for long. Those smug little tribes had better watch out. We weren't killed off by the snakes. We are warriors and we'll be looking for someone to war against very soon.

Your loving son,

Mex

The Aztecs soon turned the shallow lake into *chinampas* gardens made by piling up mud from the bottom of the lake. They built bridges and canals for transport and soon became a great trading centre. They also set about seizing power from the surrounding tribes.

The Aztecs proved to be fierce and fearless fighters.

By 1520 the Aztec emperor Motecuhzoma II ruled over a great empire in Central America. Little did he know that the Spanish were coming and the mighty Aztecs were going to fall a lot quicker than they had risen.

It's easy to think the Aztecs arrived with their special way of life and they forced the rest of Mexico to follow them. But things don't work like that. The Aztecs took control of the Toltec lands – but the Toltec religion took control of the Aztec minds!

And the Toltecs had been very bloodthirsty people. Very, very. In fact you could say very very, VERY!

The good gore guide

You know that the sun is a star ... a large celestial body composed of gravitationally contained hot gases emitting electromagnetic radiation, especially light, as a result of nuclear reactions inside the star. (No, I don't understand what it means either but it sounds good if you say it quickly.)

Anyway the Toltecs believed it was actually a god. A superhuman being who has power over human life.

Now these god people can be very tricky. If you upset them then they'll make you suffer – shine too hot on your crops, shrivel them up and starve you, or send a plague of locusts to eat all your food. The thing to do is keep your god (or gods) happy.

Some people think their god will be happy with a bit of praise and a few hymns and prayers. Other people believe they have to give prezzies to their god.

The terrible Toltecs believed you had to give a life to their god – a sacrifice.

But the awful aztecs took it to extremes. They believed they had to give their sun god human lives – thousands of them. And, not only that, they had to be sacrificed in a gruesomely gory way.

HEALTH WARNING: Readers who are sickened at the sight of a squashed rabbit on the road should NOT read this section.

The Aztecs didn't sacrifice the odd human on special occasions like the king's birthday or Bank Holiday Mondays. They did it all the time. They...

• sacrificed 50,000 a year (that's a thousand a week, six an hour or one every ten minutes!)

• sacrificed 20,000 in a single party when they opened the temple at Tenochtitlan

• had an army specially organized to keep the priests supplied with victims

• stirred up trouble among the conquered tribes so they had an excuse to go in and take prisoners who became sacrifice victims.

A Spanish history book said that when the Great Temple was opened in 1487 there were 80,000 victims sacrificed in one ceremony. But don't believe everything you read in history books! Because sacrificing 80,000 would have been just about impossible! The Aztecs would have needed machine guns and bombs to massacre that many. (In fact it's only in the past hundred years that humans have learned to kill each other at that rate – but modern people call it war and that makes it all right.)

What a way to go...

The Aztecs preferred sacrificing enemy warriors. The braver the enemy then the better the sacrifice. If an Aztec captured an enemy he would say, 'Here is my well-beloved son.' The victim would reply, 'Here is my dearest father.' You might say this sort of thing when you're asking for more pocket money! You'd better hope 'dearest' father doesn't then go on to sacrifice you.

The Aztecs had five main ways of sacrificing their victims – some more cruel than others. Which would you choose? Here's a rough guide. How would you score the methods?

1 Lie the victim on their back over the sacrificial stone, open the chest with a knife, pull out the heart and offer it to the gods in a carved stone vessel.

Score: ☆ ☆ ☆ ☆ ☆
Not bad so long as the stone isn't too cold!

- -

2 Cut off the head. This was usually the fate of female victims who'd spent some time acting the role of a goddess.

Score: ☆ ☆ ☆ ☆
A quick way to go and you'd have had a lot of fun: being treated as a goddess.

3 Tie the victim to a large rock and give him a sword club to defend himself He then fights against an Aztec warrior whose sword club has a knife edge.

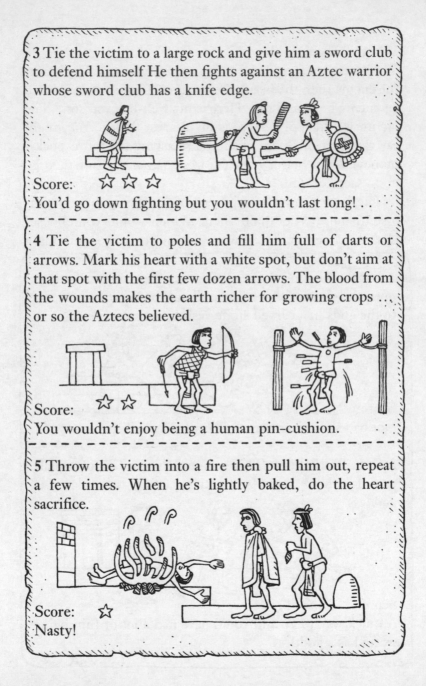

Score: ☆ ☆ ☆

You'd go down fighting but you wouldn't last long! . . .

- -

4 Tie the victim to poles and fill him full of darts or arrows. Mark his heart with a white spot, but don't aim at that spot with the first few dozen arrows. The blood from the wounds makes the earth richer for growing crops . . . or so the Aztecs believed.

Score: ☆ ☆

You wouldn't enjoy being a human pin-cushion.

- -

5 Throw the victim into a fire then pull him out, repeat a few times. When he's lightly baked, do the heart sacrifice.

Score: ☆

Nasty!

Monster mother

In 1803 Baron Friedrich Heinrich Alexander von Humboldt visited Mexico to study Aztec history. He uncovered a 3-metre high statue that weighed 12 tons. It had been carved out of a single block of volcanic stone and It was horrible. In fact it was so shocking that he buried it again!

It was a statue of the goddess Coatlicue. Victims were sacrificed in front of Coatlicue ... and after seeing her ugliness they might have died of the shock before the priests got them!

Cuddly Coatlicue was roughly human in shape but had...

• a double head of two snakes facing one another
• snakes for arms
• a cloak of snakes twisted in the wings of a vulture
• feet of a jaguar (the big cat, not the car, stupid)
• a necklace of hearts, skulls and severed hands strung together with guts.

Do you ever get bored in your school art lessons? Why not ask teacher if you can make a model of Coatlicue from modelling clay? (You don't get ideas like this on *Blue Peter*.)

When it's finished you can rip out the living heart of a jelly baby as a sacrifice. (Use a spoon for this because we wouldn't want you to cut yourself, would we?)

There is every chance that if you follow these instructions you will be expelled from your school, for being sick and disgusting. So that's another reason for doing it!

Here is cool, cute and blood-curdling Coatlicue.

Remind you of anyone?

Coatlicue's story is as gruesome as her statue. Coatlicue was a goddess and was expecting the baby who would grow up to be the sun. But before the baby was born Coatlicue was murdered by her daughter, the goddess of the moon, and her 400 sons who were the stars. They cut off Coatlicue's head - and the snakes from the neck are an image of the blood gushing out.

But the baby was born anyway and he avenged his mother's death by throwing the moon goddess off a mountain and defeating his 400 brothers. (What a baby!)

Every dawn the sun drives the moon and stars from the sky – provided he gets his regular supply of sacrifice blood, of course.

It's certain that some sacrifices ended with some bits of some victims being cooked and eaten. (The arms and the thighs were the only bits the priests allowed people to eat.) In the 1980s clever professors reckoned that the Aztecs had huge cannibal feasts – all that meat gave them the strength to fight and capture even more victims.

In the 1990s even cleverer professors say this idea is potty.

In fact the Aztecs had plenty to eat without picnicking on people …

Eat like an Aztec

Funny food

It's hard to imagine modern food without the plants discovered in Mexico 500 years ago. For example, the Maya gave us chicle – for chewing gum. And the Aztecs had other treats. What would your life be like without...

• spices ... like chilli pepper for curry

• corn ... to make your cornflakes

• pumpkin ... so Cinderella could get to the ball and you can have a hallowe'en lantern

• tomatoes ... for the sauce in your baked beans

• turkeys ... for your Christmas dinner.

The Aztecs had chocolate beans but they were so precious they were used as money. They grew peanuts that traders brought from South America. Imagine the cinema without the Aztecs – no popcorn or peanuts or chocolates.

Of course, the Mexicans didn't have cooking fat before the Spanish arrived with pigs from Europe. The Aztecs had never tasted fried food. So a great invention like chips needed potatoes (which originally came from South America) to get together with European frying before it could be enjoyed.

Ten tasty treats you wouldn't want to eat...

The people of Mexico have always had interesting food. 10,000 years ago they were driving mammoths into swamps and killing them with stone knives and spears. They would make real jumbo meals.

We can enjoy a lot of pleasant food thanks to the people of Mexico. But there are some things they used to eat that you may not be so keen to taste. Things like...

1 Monkeys – the spider monkey and the howler monkey were enjoyed by the Aztecs and are still eaten by the native inhabitants today! The howler monkey gets its name from its roar that can be heard at least 3 km (2 miles) away. If we could understand them they'd probably be howling, 'Look out! The Aztecs are coming to eat you!'

2 Toads – archaeologists found bones from marine toads in many early Mexican villages. Since the skins of these toads are poisonous they guess that they were used as a sort of drug, but too much could kill you. Wart a way to go!

3 Frogs – are safer than toads and very tasty – ask any French chef. And the Aztecs could crack awful jokes like:

4 Cactus – the maguey cactus was amazingly useful. The Aztecs used it to make needles (and the spikes) and thread, and as fuel, from paper, rope, cloth, mats and as thatching for their house roofs. The plant was boiled to give a sweet syrup and the syrup could be used to make a sort of cactus wine. The trouble was there was an Aztec law against getting drunk and the punishment was death.

5 Dogs – that's right. You wouldn't want pet pie, baked beagles on toast, Yorkshire terrier pudding or a boxer chocolate would you? Would you wolf hound after you whippet out of the oven? Surely not. The Aztecs would.

6 Lake scum – yes, the green stuff you see floating on top of the park pond. The Aztecs in Teotihuacan would collect it from the edge of the lake, press it into cakes and eat it. The trouble was the lake became polluted with chemicals used to make whitewash for the houses. Some of this scum could make an Aztec sick as a Panama parrot.

7 Lizards – tricky to catch but a very tasty bit of meat on the creatures. Nothing better than a lizard in your gizzard … it's wizard!

8 Ants - people in Europe are used to being eaten by ants when they try to picnic in a field. But the Aztecs had a better idea … they ate the ants. Lovely crunchy little snacks! Would you eat one? Perhaps one crawled into your picnic sandwich when you weren't looking! Perhaps you've already become an Aztec ant-eater!

9 Tadpoles – ask your parents about sago. It's a sort of rice-pudding dish but with clear globules that look like frogspawn. It was served regularly for school dinners – and refused regularly by children. The Aztecs would have enjoyed it because they ate tadpoles.

10 Larvae – you know what they are? Insects before they grow up. So fly larvae are known as maggots and butterfly larvae are caterpillars while beetle larvae are known as grubs.

THOSE AZTECS CERTAINLY KNOW HOW TO ENJOY THEIR GRUB!

Something you wouldn't want to drink...

The Mayans learned to make strong alcohol from the runny honey of their bees. But the honey needed bacteria (germs) to make it turn into alcohol. How did they put the germs into the honey?

Answer: Girls took the honey into their mouths, swished it around and they spat it out into a large bowl. After a few days it began to froth and bubble and turn into alcohol. But don't try this at home ... all that honey–swishing will make your teeth rot!

... and what the Aztecs didn't want to eat

Surprisingly, they didn't want to eat chocolate. The Aztecs had cacao beans from which we now make chocolate. They knew how to grind up these beans, boil them to a froth with water and sweeten the drink with vanilla and honey.

So why didn't the Aztecs drink this tasty stuff?

Because the cacao beans were too precious. For an Aztec, making a cup of chocolate would be like you eating a five-pound note sandwich … a waste of money.

Of course rich people liked to show off by drinking chocolate. They could afford it.

Food you might like to eat
Tortillas
The main food of the Aztecs would be maize which they ate with almost everything. They would make very thin maize 'pancakes', called tortillas, and use them to scoop up food from a dish or to make a parcel around some filling.

Maize flour is not common outside Mexico but ordinary flour would do. You can make about 6 tortillas with 150g of plain flour, 25g of lard and 90ml of warm water. Mix it into a dough and roll it so thin you can see the board underneath. Then heat a 20–25cm circle of dough on a flat-bottomed frying pan for about 40 seconds. It should bubble if the temperature is right. (Well, you'd bubble if you were thrown into a hot pan, wouldn't you?) Turn it over and cook the other side for about 30 seconds.

Best of all is to buy your tortillas ready-made from a supermarket!

Quesadillas

Heat a heavy frying pan till sprinkled water sizzles on it. Drop a tortilla on to the hot pan. Cover the tortilla with about 25g of grated cheese then some thin slices of onion. Lastly pop another tortilla on top. After about a minute or two the cheese begins to melt. Turn the whole thing over and heat for another minute. Eat!

You can add strips of sliced green chilli if you want a flavour of the Aztecs' favourite spice.

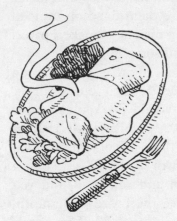

Burritos

The people of the USA call tortilla snacks 'burritos'. That means 'little donkeys' ... but don't worry, they don't have to take nuggets of Neddy from the knackers' yard. There is no donkey-meat in this at all. They are fillings of whatever you fancy wrapped in tortilla parcels.

It's a dog's life

Mexican dogs probably had very happy lives. They would not have been so happy if they knew what was going to happen to them! Luckily dogs can't see into their future. So, if you have a dog, be kind to it – don't tell it about Aztec dogs and don't leave this book lying around where Rover can read it. Because...

• The Aztecs bred small dogs for food. These dogs were practically hairless because it was so warm in Mexico ... in fact they were dogs with no ruff at all. These dogs were pot-bellied little things and Mexican potters were so fond of them they made clay models of the cute curs.

• The Maya bred dogs that didn't bark! That would give them a bit of peace and quiet at night ... but how did the poor mutts talk to one another?

• Some natives of Mexico believed a dog could help its owner to cross over into the afterlife when they died. The trouble was the dog had to be dead at the time. Whenever an owner died then the dog would be killed and buried with them. Sort of 'Spot!' Splatt!

Aztec days

Disgusting Diary

The Aztecs had a calendar of 365 days – like us but without the leap years. This calendar, and the movement of the stars and the sun, gave them a disgusting diary for the years.

The city of Tenochtitlan was massive and the twin pyramids of the Great Temple looked down on the streets. Twin pyramids to the gods – the gods of life and the gods of death ... but mainly death for the people who were conquered by the Aztec warriors.

And the streets below weren't filled with filth and rotting rubbish like the streets of Europe at that time. They were kept clean by thousands of sweepers every day. Rubbish was collected, loaded on to barges and shipped away to be dumped.

The sweepers were usually captives from other tribes who were forced to serve the Aztecs. If one of those sweepers had kept a diary then it would have been gruesome.

It may have looked something like this...

① NOVEMBER – ② NOVEMBER : DAYS OF THE PRECIOUS FEATHER

① NOVEMBER New Year. And how do the warriors celebrate? They fast – starve themselves for days on end. I'm glad I'm not a warrior who has to fast … it's bad enough being a slave. I've had my breakfast, but I'm still so hungry I could eat three dogs and still find room for a rattlesnake.

---

⑤ NOVEMBER Today the Aztecs remember the dead warriors. Well, the older warriors remember them. I would have remembered them but I forgot. Great hunting with prizes for the best hunters. Because this is the time of the hunter they take their prisoners, tie them up like deer, their front legs to their back legs. (Yes, I know people don't have front legs, but they pretend.) Then the priests sacrifice them like deer which they are really. You hear them moaning, 'Oh, deer! Oh, deer! Oh deer!' There's a lot of mess to clear up, of course. Still. It could be worse. It could be me they're sacrificing!

---

⑬ NOVEMBER This is the 'eating of the water tamales' day. They only have this once every eight years … thank the gods! The Aztecs only eat water-soaked tamales – meat and maize flour – no spices so it's like a tasteless mush. Up at the temple there are some very nice dances but the Aztecs have to go and spoil it, don't they? They end with a ceremony where they swallow water-snakes and frogs. It makes you hungry just watching them. I prefer my snake-meat roasted.

21 NOVEMBER – 10 DECEMBER : DAYS OF THE RAISING OF BANNERS

21 NOVEMBER The Aztecs celebrate the birthday of Huitzilopochtli, who grew up to beat Coyolxauhqui in battle. People wave paper flags from the houses and hang them from fruit trees! Everyone enjoys themselves … except the prisoners who get sacrificed at the Great Pyramid of Tenochtitlan. They don't complain for long.

---

11 DECEMBER – 30 DECEMBER : DAYS OF THE DESCENT OF WATER

14 DECEMBER It's wet. That's why they call these days the 'Days of the Descent of Water', because it usually rains about this time. Well, at least it's giving the pyramid a good wash down. But it's cold and muddy work out on the streets. At least it's a quiet time for the sacrifices. None of the nasty bits to sweep up.

---

30 DECEMBER – 19 JANUARY : DAYS OF THE STRETCHING

3 JANUARY The merchants pray for good trade. They sacrifice a few slaves, of course. And the priests dress up as gods and do some very nice dancing before a great feast with the lords. Of course, I never get invited to the feasts. Remind me never to become a merchant slave. I really don't want my heart ripped out of my chest – even if the Aztecs say it is a Great honour.

㉚ JANUARY – ⑧ FEBRUARY: DAYS OF GROWTH

㉖ JANUARY   Today's the day they grab the children and pull them by the neck to make them grow. Mum used to do it to me. It didn't half hurt. Still, I'm nice and tall – I've a neck like a rattlesnake, but I'm nice and tall. I held my little brother's legs while Mum pulled his head. You should have heard the neck bones creak!

㉘ JANUARY   Today the children have their ears pierced. At least, the children who survived the neck stretching have their ears pierced! I held my little brother down while our mum drilled the holes. He didn't half squawk.

㉛ JANUARY   The Aztecs honour the fire god today. Toast corn in front of his altar and toast a few animals too. Of course it's the priests who get to eat these gifts to the god. I wonder if the god ever gets hungry himself? Lots of sweeping up after ceremonies like this.

⑨ FEBRUARY – ⑬ FEBRUARY: THE USELESS DAYS

⑫ FEBRUARY　　The Aztecs have 18 months of 20 days each in their calendar. So they have these five 'useless days' left over. Everybody says they're really unlucky. (Of course no one gets sacrificed in the useless days, so I guess slaves and prisoners think they're really useful days!) And no one does any work on these days. I decided it would be best to stay in bed so the bad luck couldn't get me. But I fell out of bed. It didn't half hurt!

---

⑭ FEBRUARY – ⑤ MARCH: THE RAISING OF THE TREES DAYS

⑱ FEBRUARY　They don't really raise trees, of course. They raise poles with banners on them, then they make sacrifices to the gods of the maize and the rain. This time they sacrifice children, but at least they take them up to the mountains to sacrifice them. Less mess for me to clean up. They say the more the children cry the happier the rain god will be. If it was me I'd squawk like a parrot.

---

⑥ MARCH – ㉕ MARCH: THE FLAYING OF MEN DAYS

⑯ MARCH　　The young warriors have mock battles. Very entertaining and not too messy. But the priests make the usual sacrifices and wear the skins of the victims. I wouldn't be seen dead in a cloak of human skin myself. These Aztecs have very bad taste and they expect us slaves to clean up after them. It's a dog's life at times. (Except, of course, slaves don't get eaten like the dogs!) At least they put the skins in a holy cave in the temple. Makes a change to have priests clearing up after themselves, I can tell you. They wear those skins for 20 days. My friend cleans at the temple and says they smell dreadful!

2️⃣6️⃣ MARCH – 1️⃣4️⃣ APRIL : THE OFFERING OF FLOWERS DAYS

3️⃣ APRIL   Spring's here so the Aztecs go into the fields to sacrifice flowers! I was sweeping between the pyramids of the Great Temple today when a priest came out. He explained that the pyramids are like life and death. 'Life needs death to exist; and death needs life,' he said. I just nodded and hoped he didn't want my life! The blood doesn't half dye the steps up to the top of the pyramids. I could scrub for days and never get those stains out. I'm glad that's not my job.

1️⃣5️⃣ APRIL – 4️⃣ MAY : DAYS OF THE GREAT VIGIL

3️⃣ MAY   Young Aztec girls go in procession to bless the maize in the fields. I don't get to go, of course. More children sacrificed on the mountains. It makes you wonder how there's any children left the rate these Aztecs sacrifice them!

⑤ MAY – ㉒ MAY: DAYS OF DRYNESS

⑰ MAY It's dry. The dust in the streets is terrible and I get home filthy every night. The priests have a young man who pretends to be the god Tezcatlipoca. He has a wonderful time, him being treated like a god and all that. The trouble is gods don't get old, so they have to have a new young man every year. What happens to the old one? He gets sacrificed, of course.

㉓ MAY – ⑱ JUNE : DAYS OF EATING MAIZE AND BEANS

⑱ JUNE The end of the dry season and all that mud again. They give offerings of foods to the tools they use in the fields! I wish they'd offer some to me. They bring reeds from the lakes to make new mats, seats and decorations for the temples. There's bits of reed all over the place. Sweeping up reeds in mud isn't easy.

⑭ JUNE – ㉓ JULY: DAYS OF THE FEASTS OF THE LORDS

⑳ JUNE The lord of Tenochtitlan invites the common people to some great feasts. Of course the common Aztecs go but the slaves like me just get the job of clearing up after them. Still, there's always food left over so for once I can't complain.

24 JULY – 11 SEPTEMBER: DAYS OF THE FEAST OF THE DEAD

13 SEPTEMBER   Feasts, feasts, feasts. Any excuse. Now they're honouring the dead. These Aztecs have a good life. Apart from the sacrifices today they had this brilliant pole-climbing contest. My mum told my little brother to be careful not to win. It doesn't do to get yourself noticed. Not if you want to stay alive in Tenochtitlan!

---

24 SEPTEMBER – 11 OCTOBER: DAYS OF THE SWEEPING

1 OCTOBER   The Aztecs have a good old clean out. And where does their rubbish end up? On the streets. And who gets the job of clearing it? Me and the other sweepers. This is the time of the year when the gods return to the temples for the winter. At midnight last night the first god arrived and showed he was there by leaving a footprint in a bowl of flour in the temple. It's flour made out of maize and my mum says it's an a-maize-ing trick. She can be funny, my mum.

---

12 OCTOBER – 31 OCTOBER: DAYS OF THE FEAST OF THE MOUNTAINS

31 OCTOBER Those Aztecs have a plant called amaranth. Today they ground it up into a paste and baked it into models of the gods and snakes. But did they eat them? No! They offered them to the gods. I'll never understand these Aztecs if I live to be 50 years old. In fact I would be glad to reach 15 years old! I'm just grateful I've survived another year without getting myself sacrificed.

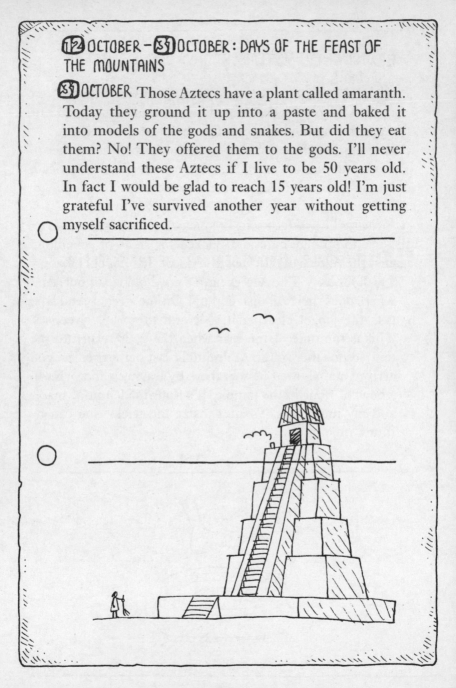

Live like an Aztec

The Aztecs were fighters. By 1500 they had conquered most of Mexico. The defeated people had to supply the Aztec homeland at Tenochtitlan with food, clothing and slaves.

But most of all the Aztecs wanted defeated warriors for their sacrifices.

Problem: How could they defeat warriors when they'd conquered Mexico and there was no one left to beat?

Answer: The Aztecs sent in spies. Aztec traders went in disguise to strange cities and looked for signs of rebellion against the Aztec rule. If they found any sign of rebel forces they encouraged it! 'Go on ... fight the Aztecs! I'll bet you could beat the loincloths off them, lads!'

As soon as the rebels went into action the Aztecs would attack and win. They would win because their trader-spies would have told them all the enemy weaknesses.

THEY ALWAYS STOP FOR TEA AT FOUR O'CLOCK

The Aztec warriors tried to capture the rebels alive so they could sacrifice them later in Tenochtitlan. That's mean and that's cheating ... but it was the Aztec way of making sure the sun kept moving in the sky.

Cruel to kids

If you wanted the gods to bring you rain or a good harvest then you had to give them gifts. You had to give them really precious gifts, of course, not just any old rubbish. What was the most precious gift they could give? A life. And what was the most precious life? The life of a child, of course. The Aztecs must have really loved children because they sacrificed dozens every year.

Of course these would usually be captured slave children. Aztecs were a bit tougher with their own children. The Aztec child was taught not to expect a happy life ... and it didn't get one! How would you like to have been an Aztec child?

THE GOOD AZTEC PARENT IS STRICT. THEN THEIR CHILD WILL GROW UP TO BE HARD-WORKING AND OBEDIENT. A USEFUL AZTEC ADULT.

FROM THE AGE OF 4 GIRLS WILL COOK AND CLEAN WHILE BOYS WILL GO FISHING OR WORKING IN THE FIELDS

THE DISOBEDIENT CHILD MAY BE PINCHED ON THE ARMS OR THE EARS

THE REALLY DISOBEDIENT CHILD MAY BE PRICKED WITH THE THORNS FROM THE MAGUEY CACTUS

Did you know...?

1 Boys were trained to be warriors. When they were baptized at a few days old they were given their warrior equipment – a miniature loincloth, a cloak, a shield and four arrows.

2 As boys grew older they were told, 'The house you were born in is not your true home – that is out there on the battlefield. Your mission is to give the sun the blood of your enemies to drink.'

3 Girls, on the other hand, were given a skirt, a blouse and weaving equipment. They were told that their place was in the home.

4 The first words a baby heard when it was born were: 'You have come to this earth which is a place of torment, a place of pain, a place of weariness, a place of illness, thirst, hunger and weeping.' Cheerful stuff. Just the sort of thing you want to hear after all the effort to get born in the first place.

AND A VERY HAPPY BIRTHDAY TO YOU TOO!

5 A child would be named after the day on which it was born. There were 20 days and 18 months but the months could have some embarrassing names. Imagine going through life as Six Dog (you'd be sick as a dog), Ten Crocodile (you'd be a bit snappy), or Eight Monkey (and if you were Aztec you would have ate monkey). Perhaps you'd prefer to be a Wind, a Vulture, a Rabbit, a Lizard, a Flower or a Death's Head?

HI, MY NAME'S 13 DEATH'S HEAD BUT YOU CAN CALL ME 'LUCKY'

6 Pottery figures of around AD 600 to 900 show Mexican native boys grinning …with their top teeth filed to a point! It probably helped them eat their roast dog But would you like to have your teeth filed? Eeeeugh!

DO YOU HAVE ANY FILLINGS?

NOPE, BUT I'VE GOT A COUPLE OF FILINGS

7 If a family was very poor then there was a quick and easy way to make some money. Sell the kids! This was an idea copied from the Maya. Slave traders would buy healthy children and take them to market. The children would have to work hard for hours on end or be punished. A bit like school, really.

HOW MANY TIMES DO I HAVE TO TELL YOU, WE AREN'T POOR, WE DON'T HAVE TO SELL YOUR LITTLE BROTHER

8 If a child died then it wouldn't get a coffin. It would be buried in a jar. Hopefully no one would later dig up the jar and mistake it for a jar of jam.

9 The Aztecs were certainly the only people in the world of the 1500s to have schooling for all boys and girls. But they didn't start school till they were 15 years old and stopped at the age of marriage – about 20. The boys could choose between schools for priests and schools for warriors. Girls generally learned singing and dancing. Then, of course, there was...

Mexican marriage

Want to marry your loved one in a genuine Aztec ceremony? This is how boys can go about it. (Sadly, girls, you don't have a lot of say in this!)

Could you survive as an Aztec? Imagine you are an Aztec boy. Try the following test.

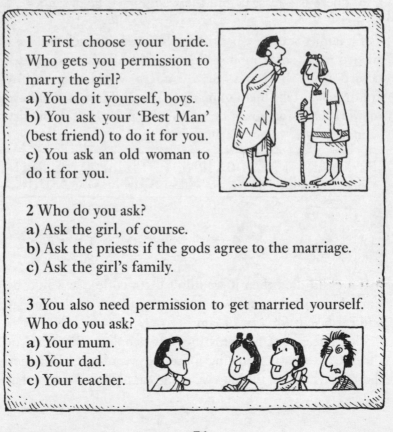

1 First choose your bride. Who gets you permission to marry the girl?
a) You do it yourself, boys.
b) You ask your 'Best Man' (best friend) to do it for you.
c) You ask an old woman to do it for you.

2 Who do you ask?
a) Ask the girl, of course.
b) Ask the priests if the gods agree to the marriage.
c) Ask the girl's family.

3 You also need permission to get married yourself. Who do you ask?
a) Your mum.
b) Your dad.
c) Your teacher.

4 How do you choose your wedding day?
a) You agree a day with your bride.
b) Everyone marries on the same day so you don't have to choose.
c) Read your horoscope and make sure it is a 'good' day on the Aztec calendar.

5 There is a feast before the wedding. Who arranges that?
a) You do it yourself, cooking food that you've hunted for yourself.
b) Your mother cooks your favourite meal with enough for everyone to share.
c) The bride's parents arrange the feast so you don't have to worry about a thing.

6 The wedding takes place after the feast and at night. How does the bride travel to your house for the ceremony?
a) In a taxi.
b) You carry her on your.
c) She is carried on the back of an old woman.

7 How do the guests get from the feast to the wedding at your house?

a) They ride on the backs of oxen.

b) They form a long line, join hands and dance from the bride's house to yours.

c) They have a torch-lit procession.

8 Everyone gives you a wedding present. When do you get your presents?

a) When you move into your new house.

b) Straight after the wedding.

c) Just before the wedding.

9 How are you joined together in marriage?

a) You and your bride each grip one end of a snake between your teeth - the boy takes the head and the girl takes the tail.

b) You simply join hands and swap rings.

c) The boy's cloak is tied to the girl's blouse.

10 There is a final feast with alcohol to drink. But only certain people are allowed to drink. Who can booze?

a) You and your friends.

b) Everyone except the bride and groom.

c) Any guests over the age of 30.

Answers: All c) answers are correct. All a) and b) answers are wrong.

1 Boys, choose your bride. It has to be someone of your own position in society. You must use an old woman as the messenger to carry your proposal. Your granny would do.

2 Ask the girl's family if you can marry her. Don't bother asking the girl herself because you don't need her permission.

3 Send your messenger to ask your teacher if you can marry! If the teacher says 'No!' then you won't be allowed.

HOW COME EVERYONE ELSE AROUND HERE HAS A CHANCE TO OBJECT EXCEPT ME?

4 Choose the wedding day. This needs to be a 'good' day on the Aztec calendar. Perhaps you could look up your horoscope in a book? Saturdays are good days.

5 The girl's family organizes a feast at her house which guests eat while she has her wedding dress and make-up put on.

6 After dinner you must wait until dark because marriages take place at night. The bride is carried on the back of an old woman to the boy's house. If your granny isn't worn out with all the running around maybe she can carry the bride.

7 Guests follow in a procession by the light of torches flaming torches, not electric torches, of course.

8 The couple sit on a mat spread in front of the fire and everyone gives them wedding presents. (Note: the Aztecs didn't have pop-up toasters, stainless steel butter dishes or electric kettles so don't give them.)

9 The couple are married when the boy's cloak is tied to the girl's blouse. This is still known today as tying the knot.

10 There's another feast (if you've recovered from the one at the girl's house!). This time the guests over the age of 30 can drink alcohol and it is no disgrace to get drunk. (Warning: Anyone under 30 getting drunk faces a beating for this crime. The next time they are caught they will be executed!)

How did you score?
10 Cheat
5 - 9 Lucky
1- 4 Get your brain cells cleaned
0 You would make a really good Aztec sacrifice

Now, boys, if you enjoyed that why not try it again with another girl ... and again with another girl ... and again with another girl. And again and again and again. How many wives can you afford?

I COULDN'T EVEN AFFORD *ONE!*

King Nezahualpilli had 2,000 wives and 144 children. How on earth did he remember their names? And, talking about kings...

The new emperor's new clothes

In Britain the monarchs have been crowned for over a thousand years in the richest robes money can buy. Thick silks, warm velvets and fur-trimmed collars. Very cosy in London fogs and Edinburgh drizzle.

The kings and queens dressed up as if to say, 'Look how grand I am, you peasants!'

But a new Aztec emperor did the opposite. He was taken in front of the sun god and had to tell the god what a feeble little human being he really was.

The emperor spent four days fasting (or three days if he was really, really fast!).

Then he took off all his clothes and stood in front of the statue of the god and said...

Oh master, oh night, oh wind, I am so poor. How can I work for this city? How can I work for its people? For I am blind, I am deaf, I am brainless and I am covered in filth. Maybe you've made a mistake and you are looking for someone else to rule?

Imagine the shock he'd get if the god said, 'All right, mate, get your kit on and push off. I'll find someone better!'

Of course all this 'humble' business didn't last long … it never does with emperors and kings. As soon as the coronation was over he went off to a feast where…

• every great lordly guest had to wear plain, simple clothes so they didn't look more grand than the emperor

• they had to bow their heads

• they were not allowed to look at emperor's face

• they were not allowed to turn their back on him so they had to walk out of his room backwards.

From then on...
• he was carried almost everywhere in a chair shaded by a canopy of precious feathers
• if he did decide to step down then nobles swept the ground in front of him and covered the ground with cloths so his feet never touched the earth
• whenever he ate he was shielded from the ordinary people by a screen of gold
• he was offered a choice of a hundred dishes of food at each meal
• he was entertained by clowns and jugglers while he ate
• he had a palace aviary with ten rooms full of birds and a palace zoo filled with animals from all over his empire – rattlesnakes were kept on a bed of feathers.

What a humble sort of life! And all he had to do was take his clothes off and admit to a stone statue he was stupid. Even you could do that!

Furious fighters

Aztec men lived to fight. When the war drum sounded every Aztec man was expected to pick up his weapons and join his group of about 800 men.

What other fantastic facts do you know about the Aztec warriors? Try this quirky quiz that Quetzalcoatl would quite quickly complete. Just answer True or False to the following…

1 Aztec warriors wore armour.

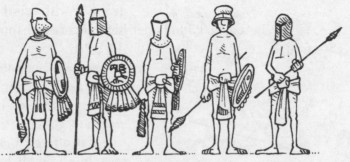

2 The Aztecs had wooden clubs, edged with stone blades that were powerful enough to cut off a horse's head.

3 Aztec leaders were easy to spot because they wore large feather and reed constructions on their shoulders.

DON'T YOU THINK THAT'S A LITTLE... WELL... TOO MUCH?

4 Aztec warriors believed that dying in battle was a wonderful thing.

5 Rich Aztec warriors wore gold and jewels when they went into battle.

6 Warriors didn't get their hair cut till they'd killed someone in battle.

7 Aztecs believed in killing themselves rather than being captured.

8 The Aztec army needed to capture 20 enemy fighters for sacrifice and no less.

9 Young Aztec men could be made full warriors by having their faces smeared with the blood of a heart that was still beating.

10 Warriors short of food would eat their dead friends.

Answers:

1 True. But it wasn't metal armour because they didn't have steel. It was a padded cotton coat, soaked in salt water to make it hard.

2 True. At least that's what the Spanish soldiers said when they fought against them. Before the Spanish arrived the Aztecs did NOT cut off horses' heads because there were no horses in Mexico.

3 True. This was fine when they were fighting other Mexican armies. But the Spanish invaders had guns and were able to pick out the leaders easily and then pick them off.

4 True. They believed that they were immediately turned into hummingbirds and hummed off to join the sun god in his heaven. Hummmm! A likely story.

5 True. Not just because they wanted to look cute as a corpse. They believed that precious stones had magical powers to protect them.

WELL, THEY'LL PROTECT HIS EARS ANYWAY

6 True. Young men had to leave some of their hair long – a disgraceful thing which told everyone that they weren't a real man yet.

7 False. King Moquiuhix tried to rebel against his Aztec friends. When his armies were defeated he threw himself off the top of his pyramid and died. The Aztec winners were so disgusted the dead king's body was not buried but left to rot.

8 True … but they sometimes took more. The Aztec Emperor Tizoc (ruled 1481 – 1486) ordered that every man in three defeated tribes should be executed. Not 20 – but 20,000.

I HOPE THEIR ARMS GET TOO TIRED BY THE TIME THEY GET TO US

9 True. Even the Tlaxcallan friends of the Spanish performed this ritual while the Christian Spanish soldiers looked on.

10 False. Warriors were happy to eat dead enemies but refused to eat the friends they had fought with, no matter how hungry they were. In the 1521 battle against the Spanish they boiled the bark of trees and ate that but left thousands of their dead friends untouched.

The gory games

The Maya played a ball game that was later copied by the Aztecs.

The Maya called it pok-a-tok, which sounds quite jolly - rather like ping-pong. The idea was that the better you played the 'ball game', the happier the gods would be and the better the crops would grow.

The ball game was linked with the ideas of human sacrifice and death. If you want to live like an Aztec then you may like to try this with a few friends. If you simply want to live … then don't ever play it!

You need:

• A court 140 metres long and 36 metres wide in the shape of an 'I'. The court is surrounded by stone walls. If that's a bit too big then try a basketball or netball court.

• A ring at each side of the court about 5 metres above the ground.

• Flat stones, carved in the shape of heads, to show the score.

• A rubber ball about 15 cm across.

• Two teams of about 10 a side – allow plenty of substitutes for players killed or carried off to hospital during the game.

• A 'skull rack' to hold the heads of sacrifice victims who'll be watching the game.

• Each player needs a helmet, and arm, knee and leg protectors made from boiled leather. (But don't go killing cows or cutting up shoes for their leather – skateboard protectors will do ... or simply don't play as rough as the Aztecs!)

The aim:

As in basketball the players of a team pass the ball among themselves till they are in a position to score. A score is made by putting the ball through one of the rings set in the wall.

The rules:

You can use arms and legs to pass the ball but you must not use hands or feet ... and that's about it really! That's probably why players were often killed during a game – there were no rules to stop you killing an opponent, and losing often meant disgrace, which made killing the opposition a very good idea. So you might want to add a rule that makes killing an opponent a foul.

The result:

The team that scores first is the winner. Some historians say losing players were taken to a platform at the side of the pitch where their heads were cut off and stuck on wooden poles. (Although you might find that a smack in the loser's face with a stale kipper may be enough of a winning celebration.) A player who scored through the hoop could claim any jewellery or clothing from the spectators. The problem was the player would have to catch the spectator first.

Sometimes the teams can agree on prizes that the winner gets. You could gamble with gold, jade, slaves or even a house ... but ask your parents before you bet your house on the result.

The truth about the ball game

Historians don't always know the truth about ancient worlds. They guess.

Most history books will tell you that the Mayan and Aztec 'ball game' was played to the death. But other historians say that is quite silly.

The truth is there were pictures carved into the walls of the ball courts. These pictures showed a ball game in which the losers lost their heads. But the pictures didn't tell the tale of a real ball game – all they did was tell the tale of a ball game that happened in an ancient legend.

So that's the story told on the walls of the ball courts. A story made up to explain why the planet Venus disappears from our skies then comes back again.

When tourists arrived in the Mayan ball courts their guides said, 'This is what happened when they played the ball game – the losers lost their heads.'

Then historians took this story and repeated it in their books. (Check your own school books on the Maya and Aztecs.) It is probably not true!

History can be horrible … but historians can sometimes be horribler.

A game you wouldn't want to try…
Volador
You need:
• A pole – tall and solid like a Maypole with a platform on top.
• Four ropes attached to the top.
• Bird costumes.
The rules:
Four players dress up as birds, climb to the top of the pole and fasten the ropes under their arms. Each bird jumps off the top of the pole and swings round it 13 times. When four players have swung round 13 times they have created the lucky number 52 and this will make sure the Sun god continues to fly around the earth.
The result:
Nothing really. Just a sort of Aztec team-bungee-jump in honour of the Sun god, and a lot less messy than heart sacrifices.

I HOPE THEY DON'T THROW UP

Foul for females

Women were not very well treated in the Aztec world. But they could do one thing that would make men respect them … they could die giving birth. That was the bravest thing a woman could do, the men said.

The unfortunate woman's ghost haunted crossroads at night. It was very unlucky to meet her. But Aztecs didn't think the dead woman's body was unlucky. Quite the opposite, they believed it had magical powers. If an Aztec warrior could just cut off a finger and some hair from her body then he could fasten it on to his shield when he went to war. The magic finger would protect him.

How did he get his hands on the fingers? Did he go to the dead woman's family and say, 'Excuse me, would you mind if I cut up her body?'

No. They were Aztecs and Aztecs never do anything so polite or simple.

When warriors heard about a suitable corpse they would get together in a gang and ambush the funeral. (Of course there couldn't be more than ten in the gang – that would make sure that everyone got a finger!)

If they missed the funeral then it still wasn't too late. They could find the grave and dig up the body!

One minute it's 'rest in peace' and the next minute it's 'rest in pieces'!

And, talking about graveyards...

Magical medicine and murderous mines

The emperor lived in his palace with some rooms large enough for 3,000 visitors. Aztec villagers lived in huts built from sun-dried bricks and whitewashed. They would have three or four rooms and enough space for 10 to 15 people to live ... and die.

Because ... when a member of the family died then they were buried under the floor of the house! This was another idea copied from the Maya. Imagine guzzling your grub over granny or sleeping over sister or drinking over Dad! Yeuch!

NOTE: This is NOT a very healthy thing to do, so don't bury your favourite goldfish under the floorboards.

If you do fall ill, then do NOT try Aztec cures. The useless ones don't work and the working ones could kill the patient. Some are still used today because the herbs worked and some seem just plain silly to us. Still, there's no harm in trying...

Curing an Aztec cold

1. FIND A CHILD WITH A COLD – THOUGH A SNEEZING TEACHER MAY DO INSTEAD

2. GET OUT OF BED AT SUNRISE AND GO TO THE NEAREST PATCH OF GRASS

3. SCOOP THE DEW OFF THE GRASS INTO A SMALL BOTTLE OR EMPTY JAM JAR

4. LIE THE PATIENT ON A BED AND TILT BACK THE HEAD

5. PLACE ONE DROP OF DEW IN EACH NOSTRIL. (YOU MAY HAVE TO CLEAR THE SNOT OUT OF THE WAY FIRST WITH A GOOD BLOW)

6. SAY A PRAYER LIKE 'OH QUETZALCOATL, DRIVE THE EVIL SPIRITS FROM THE HEAD OF THIS CHILD [OR TEACHER] AND MAKE HER [OR HIM] WELL AGAIN'

The important bit is the prayer. Most Aztec cures were aimed at driving the evil spirits from the body of the patient. Sometimes a doctor would give a really powerful drug made from morning glory flower seeds or peyote mushrooms. They could drive the patient mad or even kill them. No evil spirit with any sense would stay in a body like that!

The dead sick Aztecs

The Aztecs had no cure for diseases like smallpox that the Spanish brought from Europe. The invaders gave the Aztecs these diseases and they spread like a plague, wiping out whole villages.

One man arrived from Spain with smallpox in 1520 and killed so many Aztecs it weakened their armies and helped the Spanish to win.

Other diseases, like measles, whooping cough, yellow fever and malaria wiped out millions more. It was worse than the Black Death in Europe! If the diseases didn't get them then the exhausting work in the silver mines and the field did.

It's a mystery where the Maya went.

Where did the Aztecs go? No mystery. This is where they went...

The cunning conquistadors

Of course all of this ripping out of living hearts made the Aztecs very unpopular with the tribes that they ruled. The only hope for the suffering Mexicans lay in an ancient legend.

In this legend the Mexican people had come from another land and their leader was a god called Quetzalcoatl. This great hero had been driven from Mexico on a raft of snakes but he said he'd return one day.

The legend said that in the First Year of the Reed Quetzalcoatl would arrive with a sword and the Mexicans would recognize him because he would be a bearded white man. Quetzalcoatl would end the reign of the Aztec bullies and bring peace to Mexico.

Well, when Hernan Cortés and the Spanish landed, the legend got most of it right!

Hernan Cortés and his 600 soldiers began their conquest. With the use of guns – and with a lot of luck – they battled their way through the Aztec empire.

Crafty Cortés

Hernan Cortés set off for Mexico with 11 ships, 508 soldiers and about a hundred sailors. He also had 16 horses. The horses were going to be very important to him in battles. The people of Mexico had never seen horses before.

Cortés didn't know that the Aztecs ruled over 20 million people, but he guessed he couldn't hope to conquer the whole empire with his little army. He had to use his brains He had to win the friendship of the natives and he had to impress them with his force.

Are you as crafty as Cortés? What would you have done in these tricky situations?

The problem of the looter

Cortes had a strict rule that said his men must not steal from the defeated tribes. That was called 'looting' and was punished by death.

Shortly after Cortés had landed he began to make friends with some of the Mexican tribes who hated the Aztecs. As they marched forward some of his Mexican friends, the Zempoalans, began looting Cingapacinga villages. Cortés was angry and explained the rule against looting. 'Give back all you have taken,' he ordered.

The Zempoalans did as they were told. Cortés now had more friends – the Cingapaanga liked him too!

But then a very embarrassing thing happened. One of Cortés's own Spanish soldiers was caught looting. What could Cortés do? He was given differing advice...

A YOU HAVE TO HANG THE MAN. YOU MUST SHOW THE MEXICANS THAT YOUR LAWS ARE FAIR AND THE SAME FOR EVERYONE. THE MEXICANS MAY DESERT YOU IF YOU DON'T HANG HIM.

B YOU CANNOT HANG THE MAN. YOU NEED EVERY SPANISH SOLDIER YOU HAVE ALIVE. YOUR OWN SOLDIERS MAY DESERT YOU IF YOU HANG HIM.

They were both right! It looked as though Cortés would lose the support of his 500 conquistadors or the support of 2,000 Zempoalan warriors.

Would you follow Advice A or Advice B? Or would you accept the advice of both and lose no support at all? How could Cortés possibly do that?

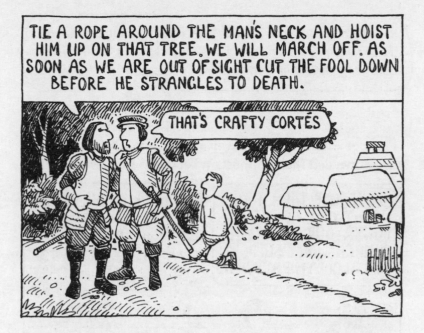

Cortés still had problems with some of his soldiers who wanted to steal a ship and sail back home. How did he solve that problem?

He burned all the ships, of course. Crafty Cortés!

The power of the priests

Cortes wanted to stop the human sacrifices – about five a day in the 'friendly' towns he was marching through. He wanted to convert the Mexicans to Christianity. The problem was that the Mexican priests were awesome men.

A Spanish writer said…

They wore black cloaks and their hair down to their waists. Some even wore their hair down to their feet, and

it was so clotted and matted with blood that it could not be pulled apart. Their ears were cut to pieces as a sacrifice and they smelled of rotting flesh.

These priests didn't want to give up their powerful positions. Cortés needed their support. What could he do?

Ⓐ EXECUTE THEM IF THEY WON'T GIVE UP THEIR POWER. OUR CHRISTIAN CHURCH WON'T SUPPORT THEIR BLOODTHIRSTY WAYS

Ⓑ IF YOU KILL THE PRIESTS THE MEXICANS WILL NOT LISTEN TO ANYONE ELSE

Would you follow Advice A or Advice B? Or could Cortés keep both the Church and the Mexicans happy?

YOU CAN STAY IN POWER BY BECOMING CHRISTIAN PRIESTS! HAVE YOUR HAIR WASHED AND CUT. HAVE A BATH AND WEAR WHITE ROBES AND WE'LL SHOW YOU HOW TO HAVE CHRISTIAN SERVICES!

And it worked. The Aztec idols were thrown off the top of the pyramid and replaced with a Christian altar and cross. The bloodstains were covered with whitewash and the pyramid priests became Christian priests – after they'd had a short back and sides, of course!

The Christians came along and said to the Aztec priests, 'Eat this bread, it is the body of our Lord and drink this wine, it is his blood!' The priests could understand this! Eating humans gave you the powers of the dead human eating bread and wine at a Christian 'communion' would give you the powers of a god! No wonder they agreed.

Cortés left the friendly towns with their converted priests and marched on to Tenochtitlan and the mighty Aztec Emperor, Motecuhzoma.

Sad superstitions

The Spanish were the winners and the Spanish wrote the history books. Like most 'winners' in history they changed the story and made up the facts to make themselves look right and the enemy look wrong.

The Spanish histories make Emperor Motecuhzoma look like a weak and stupid man who threw away his empire because he believed in silly superstitions and 'signs'.

But what were these strange signs ... and what would you have thought if you'd seen them or heard about them?

Motecuhzoma sent for his magicians and asked them to explain these terrifying signs. If you had been one of the magicians, how would you explain them?

If you were a clever magician, you'd have said…

Well? Would you have come up with the right answers? If you didn't … and Motecuhzoma's magicians didn't … then you would have suffered like them. A slow death by cruel torture.

The bad news is that there were some things that even a modern smart-Alec like you couldn't explain. Motecuhzoma also claimed to have experienced the following …

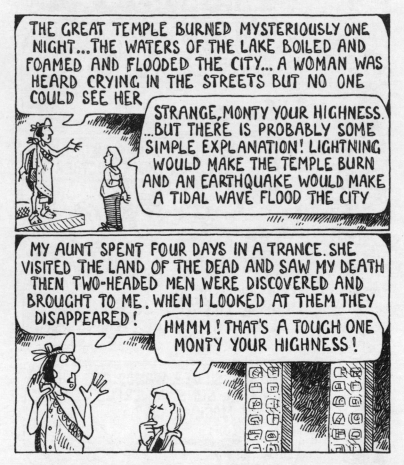

THE GREAT TEMPLE BURNED MYSTERIOUSLY ONE NIGHT…THE WATERS OF THE LAKE BOILED AND FOAMED AND FLOODED THE CITY… A WOMAN WAS HEARD CRYING IN THE STREETS BUT NO ONE COULD SEE HER

STRANGE, MONTY YOUR HIGHNESS. …BUT THERE IS PROBABLY SOME SIMPLE EXPLANATION! LIGHTNING WOULD MAKE THE TEMPLE BURN AND AN EARTHQUAKE WOULD MAKE A TIDAL WAVE FLOOD THE CITY

MY AUNT SPENT FOUR DAYS IN A TRANCE. SHE VISITED THE LAND OF THE DEAD AND SAW MY DEATH THEN TWO-HEADED MEN WERE DISCOVERED AND BROUGHT TO ME. WHEN I LOOKED AT THEM THEY DISAPPEARED!

HMMM! THAT'S A TOUGH ONE MONTY YOUR HIGHNESS!

Motecuhzoma's problem was that he didn't have enough friends to help him! The people of Tlaxcallan hated the Aztecs – not surprising since the Aztecs had spent 100 years trying to enslave them and sacrifice them. The Tlaxcallan people joined the Spanish and made Cortés's little band into an army of 5,000 warriors.

The truth is Motecuhzoma probably didn't believe Hernan Cortés was the god Quetzalcoatl on earth. The reason Motecuhzoma welcomed Cortés was that he believed he was a messenger from another great king ... which he was! Naturally he welcomed this messenger as an important visitor. Imagine the shock when the visitor entered the royal palace ... and made emperor Motecuhzoma a prisoner!

The city of horrors

Motecuhzoma had messages that Cortés and his small army had landed on the coast. The emperor tried everything to keep Cortés and the conquistadors out of Tenochtitlan, the capital city. He'd tried to bribe Cortés with gold, frighten him off with threats and kill him off with an ambush that failed.

In the end he just sat back and waited for the conquistadors to arrive.

On 8 November 1519 the Spaniard marched across the causeway to the island city of Tenochtitlan and came face-to-face with the Aztec emperor.

Cortés himself wrote down Motecuhzoma's welcoming speech...

We have known for a long time that neither I nor the people who live here are the original inhabitants. We know it belongs to strangers who come from distant parts. We always knew that they would return one day to rule us. We will obey you and all that we own is yours.

THAT'S JOLLY NICE OF YOU

Great news! The emperor himself was handing over power. The Spanish moved into the great palace of Motecuhzoma's father – and it was large enough to hold them all.

It gave the Spaniards a wonderful view, but they weren't too keen on what they saw. They looked out on the Great Pyramid for a start. A Spaniard called Tapia wrote...

> *At the top was a room with the greatest god of all the land. It was three metres high. He was made from seeds that were ground up into flour then mixed into a paste with the blood of boys and girls.*
>
> *There were more than 5,000 people in the service of this god. They rose promptly at midnight for their sacrifice which was letting blood from the tongue, the arms and the thighs, wetting straws with the blood and offering them to a huge oak-wood fire.*

Spaniard Bernal Diaz was most shocked by the 'skull rack' near the main gate to the temple. It was like a hat rack ...but for skulls. Hundreds of skulls were set in cement into a sloping wall and seventy tall poles stood on top, each pole with dozens of pegs. Diaz went on...

> *Each peg had five skulls on. A total of 136,000 skulls were counted and this did not include the countless skulls that made up the walls.*

Still, the Spaniards managed to create their own horrors in that nightmare city. A rebel chief and his sons were brought to the city for execution. Cortés ordered that they should be burned alive at the stake.

The Mexicans were used to seeing heart sacrifices by the thousand. But the whole city turned out to watch this new type of execution. They watched in silence.

Cortés had done something even Motecuhzoma hadn't managed in the city of horrors. He had shocked the Aztecs.

The angry Aztecs

Burning Mexican chiefs did not stir the Aztecs to fight against Cortés and the little Spanish force. But the Spanish made two mistakes which made the Aztecs finally rebel.

First, Cortés went into their sacrifice temple in the capital Tenochtitlan. An Indian historian described what Cortés did next.

Cortés ordered the priests to bring water to wash the blood off the walls and he told them to take the statues of their gods away. The priests laughed and said they could not move their gods. So Cortés replied, 'It will give me great pleasure to fight for my god against your gods who are nothing.' He took up an iron bar and began to smash their statues.

The priests were horrified and the Aztec people in the city were furious. The angry Aztecs may have planned to kill the Spaniards after that. They asked the conquistadors if they could hold their great harvest festival dance at the temple and invited the soldiers to watch.

The soldiers heard a rumour that the Aztecs planned to kill them straight after the dance ... so the soldiers struck first. An Indian wrote...

> They ran in among the dancers and attacked the man who was drumming and cut off his arms. They cut off his head and it rolled across the floor. Then they attacked the dancers, stabbing them, spearing them and striking some with their swords. They attacked some from behind and these fell instantly to the ground with their entrails hanging out. Some attempted to run away but their intestines dragged as they ran; they seemed to tangle their feet in their own entrails. Others they beheaded; they cut off their heads or split their heads to pieces. No matter how they tried to save themselves, they could find no escape.

Now the Aztecs organized themselves and attacked the Spaniards with huge forces. The Aztec Emperor, Motecuhzoma, tried telling his people that the Spanish were their friends. The people threw rocks and fired arrows at Motecuhzoma. A rock hit the emperor on the head and he died three days later.[1]

1. Enemies of Cortés accused him of murdering Motecuhzoma since he was no more use to him. That's probably not true. The people who wrote that weren't there at the time.

Finally the ferocious Aztecs drove the Spanish out of their capital Tenochtitlan and killed two-thirds of them – many of the Spanish drowned when they slipped into the lake because of the stolen gold they had strapped to their bodies.

The Spanish conquest of Mexico was finished after just eight months ... at least, it was finished for the moment.

Quick quiz

One of Cortés's captains, Pedro Alvarado, was fighting his way across the bridge over the lake. He was on horseback and armed with a lance. His horse was killed so he battled on with just his lance. At last he reached a place where the bridge had been broken. It was just too far for a man in armour to jump across. What would you have done ... and what did Alvarado do?

Answer: He pole-vaulted across using his lance! This sport is now part of the roadway out of Mexico City and it's still called Alvarado's leap.

Battling back

But Hernan Cortés wasn't going to give up the treasures of the Aztecs that easily. In 1521 he returned.

This was an important day in the Aztec world ... and the

Spanish world too. It would have made headline news if they'd had headlines. Or even if they'd had newspapers. You can just picture it...

el BINGO!

13 August 1521

el Sol

Just two years after landing on the filthy-rich Aztec shores, cool Conquistador Cortés (36) has captured their capital! Today his brave little army marched into the Aztec city of Tenochtitlan and he has emperor Cuahtemoc under arrest. The battle for Tenochtitlan raged nonstop for 93 days.

The battle was fierce and the wounded Cortés was being dragged to captivity by an Aztec chief. The chief stopped dragging him when Captain Olea hacked off the Aztec's arm! It was a big Aztec mistake. They had tried to take Cortés alive so they could sacrifice him. If they'd killed him when they

EXCLUSIVE:
HAPPY HERNAN GOES FOR GOLD

had the chance then the Spaniards could have lost the whole war.

A tired but happy Cortes told our reporter, 'My men did well. When we landed here we had no idea the place was so big. Otherwise we might have given up before we even started!'

The Spanish fought bravely because they saw what happened to their comrades who were captured. They watched in horror as Spanish prisoners were dragged to the top of the temple pyramid, had their beating hearts ripped out and their bodies kicked down the steps to butchers waiting below.

Footsore soldiers agreed. 'We were all for going home as soon as we got here,' Private Christofer Robino (24) agreed. 'But Captain General Cortes burned our boats so we had to go forward. Unless we wanted to sail back to Spain on a lump of charcoal!' he laughed.

Hoards of Aztec treasure are awaiting the clever conquerors but first they have to clean up the city. Our reporter says it is an amazing place, built on an island and surrounded by farms on artificial islands. There are about 200,000 people living in the city and as many as 60,000 come to the Tenochtitlan market from all over the empire. The peasants live in wood and mud houses but the nobles and priests live in fine stone palaces.

But the real horror hovers in the centre. The city centre is dominated by the temples – huge stepped pyramids, plastered with brilliant colours. But the colours are stained by crusted dried blood and the stench of death in the midday sun has turned the stomachs of the strongest soldiers.

Captain-General Cortés has big plans for terrible Tenochtitlan and its awful

Aztec cannibals. He is planning to convert the natives to Christianity then he'll flatten the evil city to the ground. 'If the Indians don't convert to Christianity then we'll torture them and execute them until they do,' he said grimly. 'That'll put a stop to all this cruel killing.'

Hernan Cortés was made Governor of the country, which was renamed New Spain. The Aztecs had been rubbed out of history; the Spaniards destroyed their great capital of Tenochtitlan utterly, the Spanish priests destroyed the Aztec statues, their libraries and their picture-writings.

Cortés then sent one of his generals, Francisco de Montejo, to conquer the tribes who remained in the old Mayan kingdom. By 1546 the northern Mayan cities had been defeated with dreadful slaughter and half a million Maya were sold into slavery. The Itza tribe hid in the dense jungles and stayed free until 1697. Then the Spanish arrived and crushed this last tribe of old Mexico.

Of course the killing didn't stop when Cortes defeated the Aztecs. The Aztec peasants became slaves and were worked to death by the Spanish conquerors. Spanish settlers took over the Aztec lands – the Spanish priests converted the Aztecs to Christianity: the great bloodstained pyramids were pulled down and the rubble from them used to build a Christian cathedral. The sacrifices stopped ... but people carried on being killed.

Conquistadors conquered

You may be pleased to hear that the Spanish conquistadors didn't have it all their own way. Stealing the treasure of the

Aztecs was easy compared to their next task … getting it back across the Atlantic to their king in Spain.

Three fat, slow transport ships set off from Mexico in 1523. Conquistador Cortés wrote:

> *I am sending you things so marvellous that they cannot be described in writing, nor can they be understood without seeing them*

These 'marvellous things' included jaguar and puma cats, sugar, emeralds, topazes, carved masks encrusted with jewels, feathered cloaks of Aztec priests, red–yellow–blue macaws, talking parrots, Aztec slaves, rings, shields, helmets, vases and polished stone mirrors. The pearls alone weighed 300 kg and there was 220 kg of gold dust, three huge cases of gold ingots and other cases of silver bars.

The gold and silver never made it to Spain … and neither did some of the Spanish conquistadors as extracts from the ship's log show…

Day 17	Sickness has killed eleven of our crew in the first two weeks. Weather bad, ship leaking and progress slow.
Day 24	Storm smashed wooden cage last night. Jaguar escaped. Beast tore arm off one sailor, ripped leg off soldier and clawed open shoulder of third before it leapt overboard. Two men died. Officers elect to

> shoot the other jaguar in its damaged cage.
>
> **Day 87** Reached Azores. Commander Quixones went ashore with officers but returned quarrelling about a woman they had met. Officer split Quixones, skull with his cutlass. Commander Quixones, body thrown overboard for sharks and brains washed off deck with sea-water.
>
> **Day 133** French pirates have damaged two of our ships and boarded them. Only this ship will ever reach Spain. We tried to fight but our powder is defective after months at sea. King Carlos will not be pleased.

King Carlos was furious. But for the next 200 years the Spanish would have to get used to being robbed by pirates waiting, like vultures, to tear the riches from the treasure ships.

The Quetzalcoatl quiz

Now that you know everything your teacher never knew about the Aztecs, you can torture Sir or Miss even more. No, not by ripping out their heart with a stone-age knife. By testing their brain cell with these fiendishly foul questions. (If you can't torment a teacher then pester a parent – and if your parents run screaming you'll just have to test yourself!)

1 What sort of knife did the priests use to cut out a victim's heart?
a) glass
b) bronze
c) gold

2 The name Quetzalcoatl means what?
a) white man with beard
b) a coat decorated with quartz stones
c) a snake with feathers

3 Before the Aztecs came the Toltecs and before the Toltecs came the Olmecs. The Olmecs were known as what?
a) the green monkey people
b) the rubber people
c) the cactus-haired people

4 Aztec children were given the job of collecting things in the fields. What did they collect?
a) berries
b) beetles
c) bat droppings

URGH LOOK! BAT DROPPINGS WITH BEETLE-BERRIES IN THEM

5 Aztecs were told what to wear. Poor people wore simple clothing and lords wore rich clothing. What was the punishment for a poor person caught wearing rich clothes for a second time?

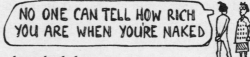

NO ONE CAN TELL HOW RICH YOU ARE WHEN YOU'RE NAKED

a) death
b) being stripped
c) having their house knocked down

6 The Aztecs asked the Spanish conquerors if they could go to their temple for a harvest festival dance. The Spanish agreed. What happened when the Aztecs arrived?
a) They were preached to by Christian priests.
b) They were told that sacrifices in the temple were banned from now on.
c) They were massacred.

7 The Aztec traders became very rich and dressed in fine clothes. But the emperor would have hated this. So what did they do?

a) They had to wear a plain white cloth over the top of their fine clothes. It reached down to their ankles.
b) They wore a reversible coat. It was rich on the outside but they could turn it round quickly if the emperor appeared to show a plain side.
c) They had to creep into the city at night so no one, especially the emperor, could see them.

8 When the Spanish arrived in Mexico they noticed little wooden huts on the side of the road in both the country and the town. Aztecs popped in for a couple of minutes before coming out again looking content. What were the little wooden huts?
a) public toilets

b) Aztec national lottery shops

c) Aztec pubs for drinking maize wine

9 How did Aztecs keep their teeth clean?
a) They had toothpicks made from cactus spines.
b) They used chewing gum.
c) They made toothpaste from powdered stone in cream.

10 The Spanish discovered the Aztecs had lots of gold and they tricked them out of it by saying, 'We need your gold...'
a) '...to give to the poor and the hungry natives.'
b) '...to make you metal guns like ours which we'll give you for hunting.'
c) '...because it's the only thing that will cure you of your disease.'

Answers:
1a) The knives were made of a type of natural glass that came from hardened volcanic lava. It is called 'obsidian' and can be polished to look really sharp, shiny and attractive. It's used to make jewellery now.

SEE, IT'S A CUTE LITTLE DAGGER

2c) Quetzalcoatl was a serpent or snake with plumes or feathers. How could the Aztecs mistake a Spanish soldier for a snake with feathers? They must be a bit shortsighted. No wonder the Spanish beat them so easily!
3b) The Olmecs were NOT called the rubber people because they were like bendy toys. They got their name because they lived in the area where rubber trees grew until the Toltecs rubbed them out, of course. No one knows what name the Olmecs called themselves.
4b) The Aztec children collected female scale beetles that live on cactus plants. These beetles were crushed and used to make red dye for clothes, called cochineal.

The Spanish invaders brought the idea back to Europe and it is still used in places as food dye. The Aztecs needed 150,000 beetles to make one kilo of dye. The Aztecs dyed – the beetles simply died.

5a) A peasant trying to pose as a posh person had their house knocked down the first time they were caught. If they tried it again they would be executed. And you thought school uniforms were a rotten idea?

I'M JUST TAKING IT TO THE CLEANERS! HONEST!

6c) The Spanish killed them. And, as we've seen, this made the surviving Aztecs angrier and fight even harder to throw out the Spanish bullies.

7c) The merchants had to creep around after dark when they returned from trading. There was another way to keep them fairly poor and a little more humble. The richer they were the greater the feasts they had to give to the nobles. They were forced to give rich presents to their guests ... and buy fine slaves in the market to be sacrificed. Imagine having a birthday party where you give all the presents!

8a) The Aztecs needed human 'manure' to spread on their fields so they encouraged people to use public toilets. The toilets would be emptied on to the soil to make it richer and help the pumpkins and maize grow better. But don't worry - your cornflakes won't have been grown with human manure ... probably just lots of chemicals, weed-killers and pest-killers. Haven't things improved since Aztec times?

9b) Aztecs chewed chicle gum made from a milky fluid inside some trees and plants. It is still used for chewing gum today. Some things never change. The Aztecs didn't like people who chewed in public and especially those who made popping and snapping noises with the gum … just like some children do in their classrooms! And today's teachers don't like that either. Something else that hasn't changed!

10c) The sad Aztecs believed that the Spanish conquerors would use the gold to cure them of the diseases that had come from Europe. What was this disease supposed to be? Gold fever?

Epilogue

Some historians try to make excuses for the Aztecs. They say, 'The Aztecs lived in violent times and had to be ruthless and bloodthirsty to survive.'

That may have been true at the start of their rise to power. But they began to enjoy the cruelty. That is harder for us to forgive ... and it led to their downfall in the end.

When Emperor Tizoc wanted a sacrifice he believed that he needed 20 warriors to die on the pyramid in Tenochtitlan. Instead he decided to terrify all the other tribes in Mexico with a huge massacre. He took every single man from three Mixtec tribes, 20,000 men, and sent them for sacrifice.

The victims had eagle feathers stuck to them with their own blood and were led to the Aztec capital. They were all killed on the pyramid. The Aztecs killed the first ones then the priests took over. In early sacrifices the people had eaten small parts of the victims. This time there were too many. They were simply killed and their bodies thrown into the marshes.

It terrified the other tribes in Mexico all right. But it also disgusted them. They learned to hate the Aztecs. They knew they would have to wait, but one day their chance would come to overthrow the vicious, heart-ripping people.

And that chance came when the Spaniards arrived. If the Aztecs had been popular then all the people of Mexico would have joined together to drive them back to Spain. Instead they turned against the Aztecs and destroyed them. Sadly the Spaniards just said, 'Thanks very much!' and took over from the terrors of Tenochtitlan.

An Aztec poem moaned ...

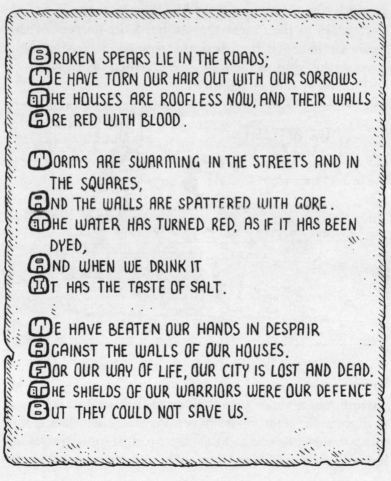

BROKEN SPEARS LIE IN THE ROADS;
WE HAVE TORN OUR HAIR OUT WITH OUR SORROWS.
THE HOUSES ARE ROOFLESS NOW, AND THEIR WALLS
ARE RED WITH BLOOD.

WORMS ARE SWARMING IN THE STREETS AND IN
   THE SQUARES,
AND THE WALLS ARE SPATTERED WITH GORE.
THE WATER HAS TURNED RED, AS IF IT HAS BEEN
   DYED,
AND WHEN WE DRINK IT
IT HAS THE TASTE OF SALT.

WE HAVE BEATEN OUR HANDS IN DESPAIR
AGAINST THE WALLS OF OUR HOUSES.
FOR OUR WAY OF LIFE, OUR CITY IS LOST AND DEAD.
THE SHIELDS OF OUR WARRIORS WERE OUR DEFENCE
BUT THEY COULD NOT SAVE US.

The hideously bloodstained pyramid in Tenochtitlan was blown up with 500 barrels of gunpowder. A Christian cathedral was built in its place. Things should have started to improve for the suffering Mexicans. But history is too horrible to allow 'happy ever after' endings.

Those Mexicans had slaved in the fields and died for the Aztecs. Now they slaved in the fields and died for the Spanish conquistadors – if the Mexicans were late in paying their taxes to the Aztecs they suffered the horrors of the heart sacrifice – if the Mexicans were late in paying their taxes to the Spanish then they were burned to death.

Either way they ended up dead.

Rebels in the south of Mexico tried digging pits with sharp stakes to stop the charging Spanish horsemen ... the conquistadors threw the rebels on to their own stakes.

Rebels in other Spanish regions had their hands cut off but were allowed to live – the Spanish hung the hands around their necks and said, 'Go and show your people what happens to rebels.' And the conquistadors called the Aztecs savage!

The Mexicans had a good way of looking at death. A poem in the old Aztec language of Nahuatl puts it best. It said...

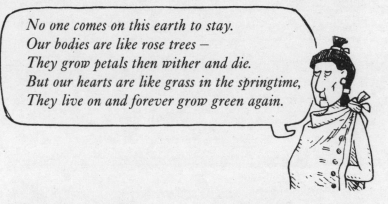

No one comes on this earth to stay.
Our bodies are like rose trees —
They grow petals then wither and die.
But our hearts are like grass in the springtime,
They live on and forever grow green again.

People come and go. So do nations. The Olmecs, the Toltecs, the Aztecs. All gone.

And, if you believe the ancient Mexican legends, the earth itself comes and goes. On 22 December 2012 it will be destroyed yet again.

Or will it? History can sometimes be horribly wrong! We'll just have to wait and see.

ANGRY AZTECS

GRISLY QUIZ

**Now find out if you're a
angry Aztec expert!**

HORRIBLE HABITS

The people of Central America had some horrible habits. How much have you learned about their beastly beliefs?

1. What did the Mayans do to enemy peasants captured during their wars?
a) Made them slaves
b) Sacrificed them to the gods
c) Boiled them with herbs and ate them for supper

2. What did Mayan priests wear to dance in during sacrifices?
a) Grass skirts decorated with sequins
b) Nothing
c) The skin of their enemy leaders

3. Which of the following was not a method used by the Aztecs for sacrificing victims?
a) Pulling out their heart
b) Throwing them in a fire
c) Beating them over the head with the altar stone

4. The Aztecs were big dog breeders (I mean they liked to breed dogs, not that the dogs were big!). Why?
a) The dogs could keep watch for enemies
b) Dogs made tasty snacks
c) The Aztecs had a soft spot for pet pooches

5. What did the Aztecs do during the Days of Growth?
a) The pulled children by the neck to make them grow
b) They did a dance to make the crops grow
c) They built their pyramids even higher, trying to reach heaven

6. Where did the Aztecs bury their dead?
a) Under the floorboards
b) In the temples
c) They didn't – they burned them

7. What does Teotihuacan mean?
a) The place where enemies are sacrificed
b) The place where gods are born
c) The place where chocolate is eaten

8. Why did the Mayans chuck little girls into wells?
a) So they could speak to the gods
b) So they could see how deep the well was
c) The girls were thirsty

AMAZING EMPERORS

The Aztec emperors were a strange bunch. They ruled ruthlessly (you didn't make one angry if you wanted to keep you heart in your chest) but helped bring power to their people. Take this quick quiz and see how much you know about these evil emperors.

1. Who was the first Aztec emperor? (Clue: It's a capital name)
2. What did the emperor Itzcoatl order to be burned during his reign? (Clue: No more horrible history!)
3. Who did Motecuhzoma II think Hernan Cortés was when the Spaniard appeared in Tenochtitlan? (Clue: No mere mortal)
4. What did Motecuhozoma I bring to the city of Tenochtitlan during his reign? (Clue: What-a great idea!)

5. What were first created during the reign of Acamapichtli? (Clue: New rules)

6. Which industry improved during the reign of Huitzilhuitl? (Clue: It makes (fashion) sense)

7. How did Chimalpopoca die? (Clue: Come on, don't leave me hanging…)

8. What did Hernan Cortés do to the leader Cuauhtemoc? (Quite the opposite of having cold feet!)

FRIGHTENING FIGHTERS

Could you have made an awful Aztec warrior? Here are a few foul facts about the ferocious Aztec fighters – but you have to fit in the missing words.

Missing words, not in the correct order: *salt water, feather, humming, birds, precious stones, priests, arrows, enemy fighters, heart, blades, friends*

1 AZTEC BOYS WERE GIVEN A MINI LOINCLOTH, SHIELD, CLOAK AND FOUR ____ WHEN THEY WERE A FEW DAYS OLD.

2 ALL AZTEC BOYS WENT TO SCHOOL AT 15 AND COULD CHOOSE TO BE TRAINED AS WARRIORS OR AS ____.

3 YOUNG MEN COULD BE MADE FULL WARRIORS BY HAVING THEIR FACES SMEARED WITH THE BLOOD OF A ____ THAT WAS STILL BEATING.

4 AZTEC WARRIORS WORE PADDED COTTON 'ARMOUR', WHICH WAS SOAKED IN ____ TO MAKE IT HARD.

5 THE AZTECS WERE ARMED WITH POWERFUL WOODEN CLUBS, EDGED WITH STONE ____.

6 RICH AZTEC WARRIORS WORE ____ THAT THEY BELIEVED HAD MAGICAL POWERS TO PROTECT THEM IN BATTLE.

7 WARRIORS SHORT OF FOOD WOULD EAT DEAD ENEMIES BUT WOULD NEVER EAT DEAD ____.

8 THE AZTEC ARMY NEEDED TO CAPTURE AT LEAST 20____ FOR SACRIFICE.

9 AZTEC WARRIORS BELIEVED IF THEY DIED IN BATTLE THEY WOULD TURN INTO ____ AND GO TO HEAVEN.

10 AZTEC LEADERS WORE LARGE STRUCTURES MADE OF ____ AND REEDS ON THEIR SHOULDERS.

AZTEC FACT OR FICTION

Many mysteries surround the angry Aztecs and horrible historians still don't know the whole truth about their crazy culture. Here are a few surprising statements. Can you tell which are true and which are false?

1. The Aztec punishment for being drunk was to have your head shaved.

2. Aztec children started school at the age of five and left when they were 10.

3. When a boy was born, his umbilical cord was cut and buried on a battlefield.

4. Naughty Aztec kids were punished by being held over a fire of chilli peppers.

5. To cure earache, Aztec doctors would drop fresh dew in the patient's ears.

6. When the Europeans arrived, the Aztecs ruled over more than 20 million people.

7. Aztec men could have as many wives as they liked.

8. The Aztecs loved the game of tlachtli (pok-a-tok) so much that they used thousands of balls from the Maya.

Horrible habits
1a; 2c; 3c; 4b; 5a; 6a; 7b; 8a

Amazing emperors
1. Tencoch. He was a chief chosen to become emperor.
2. The codices (a type of Aztec book) that recorded their history and myths.
3. The god Quetzalcoatl.
4. Water – he completed an aqueduct pipe system in the capital.
5. It is believed that the first laws were introduced during his reign (1376–95).
6. Weaving – suddenly the Aztecs were comfy in cotton.
7. He hung himself by his belt after being captured by an enemy tribe.
8. Tortured him by putting his feet in a fire!

Frightening fighters
1) arrows 2) priests 3) heart 4) salt water 5) blades 6) precious stones 7) friends 8) enemy fighters 9) humming birds 10) feathers

Aztec fact or fiction

1. True. At least, that's what happened the first time you were found singing in the gutter. If it happened again you were punished by ... death!

2. False. They didn't start until they were 15 (lucky Aztecs!) and they stayed until they were 20.

3. True. This was to show that his life would be devoted to war.

4. True. But you'd have to have done something reeaaally bad to have this done to you (like skiving your horrible history lesson).

5. False. That was the cure for colds. For earache they put liquid rubber in the ears, of course!

6. True. And not many of their subjects were sorry to see them squashed by the Spaniards!

7. True. In fact the more the merrier, as the wives weaved cloth that could be sold to make the families very rich.

8. True. The Aztecs stole the idea of the game from the Maya, and got them to supply more than 15,000 balls a year!

INTERESTING INDEX

Where will you find 'eating scum', 'drinking spit' and 'gut necklaces' in an index? In a Horrible Histories book, of course.

Terry Deary was born at a very early age, so long ago he can't remember. But his mother, who was there at the time, says he was born in Sunderland, north-east England, in 1946 – so it's not true that he writes all *Horrible Histories* from memory. At school he was a horrible child only interested in playing football and giving teachers a hard time. His history lessons were so boring and so badly taught, that he learned to loathe the subject. *Horrible Histories* is his revenge.

Martin Brown was born in Melbourne, on the proper side of the world. Ever since he can remember he's been drawing. His dad used to bring back huge sheets of paper from work and Martin would fill them with doodles and little figures. Then, quite suddenly, with food and water, he grew up, moved to the UK and found work doing what he's always wanted to do: drawing doodles and little figures.